Main Activity:

Problem Solved!

BOOK 1

Brian Fillis

Badger Publishing

Contents

Section One: Solve problems and investigate

1 Problems involving money 04
- A Money problem bank

2 Problems involving percentages 11
- A How much off? – You decide
- B Flags

3 Problems involving ratio and proportion 19
- A Timetables
- B Ratio problem bank
- C Populations

4 Problems involving number and algebra 28
- A Number cards
- B Sum puzzles
- C Consecutive integers
- D Shape expressions

5 Problems to solve with a graphical calculator 38
- A Investigate the calculator: sequences
- B Draw shapes

6 Problems involving shape and space 45
- A Dominoes, Quadrominoes, Pentominoes
- B Shape and space problem bank

7 Problems involving perimeter and area 58
- A Congruent shapes
- B Two shapes

8 Problems involving measures 67
- A Measure problem bank
- B Motorway junctions

9 Problems involving probability 74
- A Spinners
- B Cards

10 Problems involving handling data 83
- A Mean puzzles
- B The population of the UK: ethnic groups

Section Two: Using and applying maths to solve problems

1 Problem solving 93

- A Nonsense words
- B What's the problem?
- C Check your answers

2 Reasoning 99

- A Venn diagrams
- B True, false and it depends...
- C What if... ?

3 Communicating 106

- A Explain your answer
- B Jumbled explanations

Monica

Hussein

Neil

Ki

Viu

1 Problems involving money

A Money problem bank

1. Ki bought a £4.99 book, a £1.30 magazine and a 92p pen.
   What was the **total** cost?

2. Neil buys a scientific calculator for £8.65.
   He pays for it with a £20 note.
   How much change should he receive?

3. Viv has five 20p coins and three 50p coins.
   He pays £1.35 for a 'Get Well' card.
   How much money does he have left?

4. | | | | | |
   |---|---|---|---|---|
   | Pencils cost: | 18p | 32p | 50p | 65p |
   | Pens cost: | £1.02 | £1.14 | £1.68 | £1.85 |

   Hussein buys a pen and a pencil.
   He pays **exactly** £2.
   Which pencil and pen did he buy?
   Explain how you worked it out.

5. The magazine 'Tuffy the Vampire Dentist' costs £2.15. Ki saves 60p a week.
   How many weeks must she save to buy the magazine?
   How much will she have left?

6. Monica bought **12 packets** of ink pens.
   Each packet costs £4.60.
   How much did Monica pay for the packets altogether?

7. Viv paid **£6.58** for some boxes of pencils.
   Each box cost **47p**.
   How many boxes did Viv buy?

8 Look at the packets.
How much does **one** rubber cost? **One** ruler? **One** pair of compasses?

9 The shopkeeper has four cheques in the till.
The amounts on the cheques are:
£6, £3.50, £1.75 and £2.99.
She decides to add up the total in her head.
Explain how **you** would work it out in your head.
What is the total?

10 Neil saved 35p a week for a whole year.
How many pounds did he save in total?

11 A small bottle of Pledge's Pop costs £1.10.
The larger bottle costs **one and a half times** as much.
How much does the larger bottle cost?
Show your working out.

12 Monica has £15.
She buys two magazines.
Each magazine cost £2.35.
She spends £1.40 on bus fares.
How much money does she have left?

13 Neil buys three packs of stickers.
He gives the shopkeeper a £5 note.
He gets £2.90 change.
What is the cost of **one** packet of stickers?
Explain how you worked it out.

14 Viv and Ki buy one lottery ticket each.
They agree that if one of them wins a prize,
they will share it equally. Ki wins £37.50.
What should each friend get?

15 Monica buys **two** lottery tickets and Hussein buys **one**.
They agree that if one of them wins a prize,
they will share it.
Monica wins £51.

Monica

Hussein

How should the friends split their prize?
How much does Monica get?

16 The prices of magazines are:

Tuffy the Vampire Dentist	£2.15
Dull-Pop Weekly	85p
Footballer's Haircuts	£1.30
The Economist	£2.50

Viv buys two magazines.
He pays £10 and receives £6.55 change.
Which two magazines did he buy?

17 £1 is worth 1.4 Euros.
A CD costs £5.
How much would it cost in Euros?
Show your working.

18 £1 is worth 1.6 US dollars.
A book costs £6.99. **Approximately** how much would it cost in US dollars?
Show your working.

19 Neil bought a protractor and a pair of compasses. He paid 90p in total.
Monica bought **two** protractors and a pair of compasses. She paid £1.25 in total.
What is the cost of a pair of compasses?

20 All five friends go to a theatre to see 'Mother Gap's Dolly House'.
The total cost of the tickets is £21.
How much would it cost **six** people to see the play?

21 Hussein is at a print shop, having his data handling project printed from a disc.
He wants the project to be put in a special binder when it's printed.
This is what the shop charges for printing and binding:

Printing:	**4p per page**
Binder:	**£1.20**

Hussein pays £2.12 in total.
How many pages are there in his project?

22

a The cost of a ticket to see the film 'Hannah and her Lawyers' is £1.40.
On Tuesday, **180 people** pay to see the film.
How much money is that altogether?
Show your working – don't use a calculator this time.

b On Wednesday, the cinema takes **£700** in ticket sales.
How many people paid to see the film on Wednesday?
Show your working – again, try to work it out without the calculator.

23

'Howell's Electrics' is selling the new Y-Box games console for £120. They have a sale and cut the normal price by 15%.
How much will it cost now?

24 At 'McKinley's' the Y-Box normally costs £170. They have a sale and cut the normal price by $\frac{1}{4}$.
At which shop would you buy the Y-Box?
Explain why.

25 The newsagent's sells pens in two different packs:

Which pack is best value for money?
Explain your reasoning.

26 Neil gave some money to the school charity fund.
Viv decided to give twice as much as Neil.
Ki gave £6.
Altogether, the three friends gave £18 to the fund.
How much did Neil give?
Show your working.

27 Neil bought two DVDs and one CD.
The total cost was £30.
Viv bought one DVD and three CDs.
The total was £35.
What is the cost of one DVD?

28 In 1971, the money used in the UK was changed by the government. The change was called 'decimalization'.
What do you think the name means?

Before decimalization, the pound was a note, not a coin. The most common coins used were the shilling, the sixpence and the penny. There were 20 shillings in the pound. There were 12 pennies in the shilling. One shilling was equivalent to today's 5p. There was a sixpence coin which was equivalent to 2.5p.

Prices were given in the form: '£3/12/6' which means 3 pounds, 12 shillings and 6 pence. The shopkeeper would call this price 'three pounds twelve and six.'

This fridge cost 7,182 pennies in 1968.
Prices have risen by roughly 1000% over the last 30 years.
What would a similar fridge cost today?

Problems involving percentages

A How much off? You decide

1

a The shopkeeper increases the price of the TV set by 20%. Work out the new price. Show your working.

b The shopkeeper has reduced the price of the DVD player. What is the reduction **as a percentage**?

2

Clock-radio: £14

Widescreen TV: £398

DVD player: £180

Video recorder: £68

Midi-system: £249.50

Digital camera: £120

Mini-disc player: £85

Mini-turntable: £49.99

CD walkman: £29.75

MP3 player: £370.20

CD radio-cassette: £73

Digital TV box: £104

Imagine that you own an electrical shop and you decide to have a sale.
Choose a percentage from the target board.
Choose **four** items from the drawing that you are going to **reduce**.

Work out the sale price of your four items **after** your reduction.
Show your working out, even if you decide to use a calculator.

3

What is the price of the DVD now?
What is the price of the video recorder?

Who is right? Can you explain why?

4

Who is right – Viv or Ki? Explain why.

❺ The rival sale

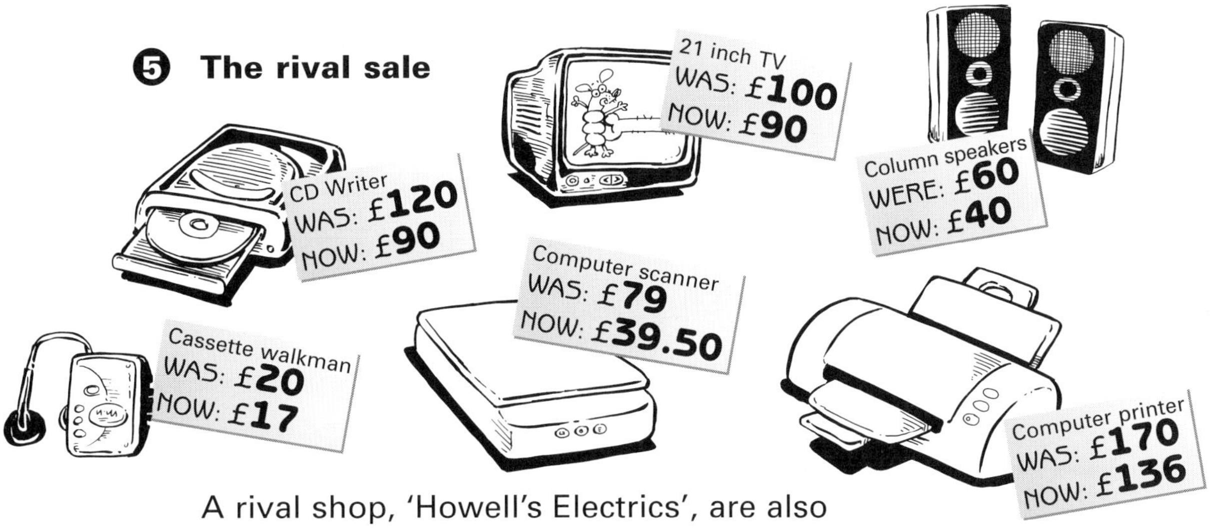

A rival shop, 'Howell's Electrics', are also having a sale.
By how much has the CD-writer been reduced?

a What is the **percentage reduction** on the CD writer? Explain how you know.

b

The shopkeeper has percentage reduction stickers to put on the items. Choose at least two stickers and decide which item they should be stuck to. Explain how you worked it out.

❻ Customer enquiries

THE LAMP
A customer comes to the shop. She says:
"You're charging **£48** for the lamp.
I saw it on sale at 'Howell's' for £36!"
You decide to use a percentage to reduce the price of the lamp.
Which percentage should you use to make the lamp the **same price** as 'Howell's'?
Which percentage will make it **cheaper** than 'Howell's'?

THE TOASTER
A customer enters the shop. He says:
"I notice you're selling the toaster for £40.
Did you know 'McKinley's' are selling it for £32?"
Which percentage reduction will make the toaster the same price as 'McKinley's'?
Which percentage reduction will make it less than 'McKinley's'?
How much less will it be? Show your working.

THE CD PLAYER
A customer storms into the shop.
"Where is the manager?" she bellows.
"'Copley's' are selling that CD player for £139.75.
You're charging £215!"
Which percentage reduction will make the CD player the same price? Show your working.

The CD player cost **you** £130 to buy from the manufacturers.
You decide to reduce the CD player from £215 so that you will only make £1 profit.

What percentage reduction will you offer?

7 The shopkeeper **reduced** the price of the phone **by 10%**.
One week later, he decided to end the sale and **increased** the price by **10%**. What is the price of the phone now?

Who is right? Can you explain why?

8

This record deck has been reduced by 15%.
The sticker shows the price that you are asking for it **now**.
What was the price **before** you reduced it?

Viv is **wrong**.

Yes he is.
What maths can we do to show Viv that he's wrong?

B Flags

HMS Rectangle

1

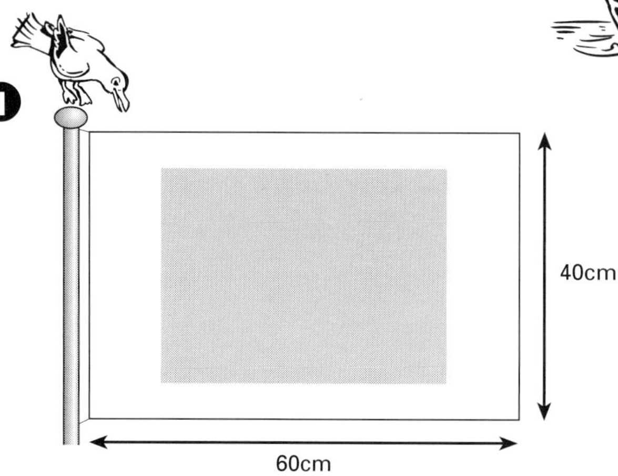

a 50% of this flag is shaded.
What is the **area** of the shaded rectangle?

b The length of the shaded rectangle is 40cm.
What is its width?

2

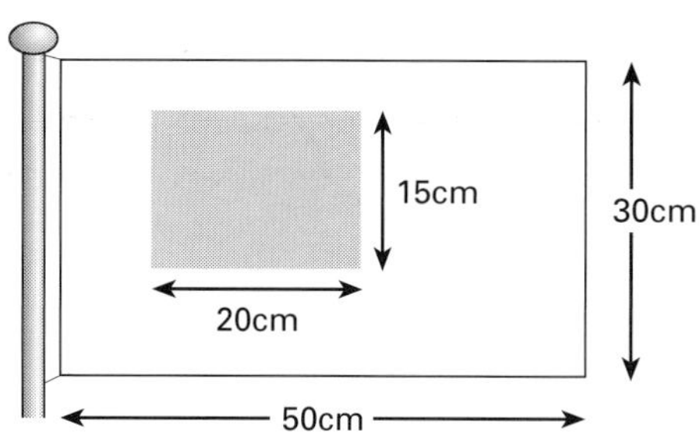

What percentage of this flag is shaded?

3

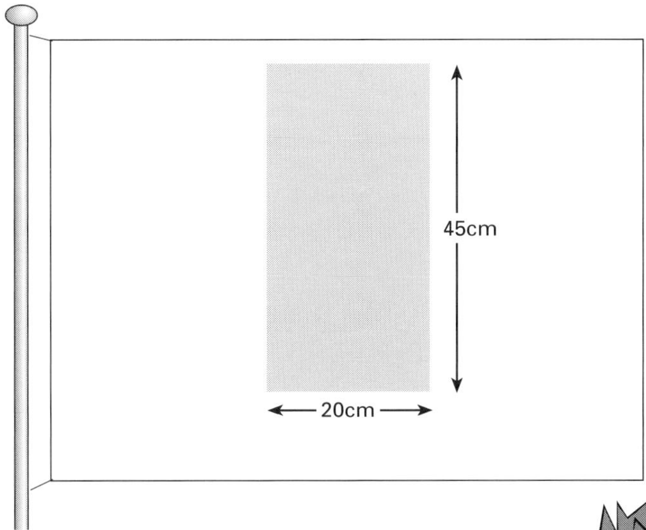

a 25% of this white flag is shaded.
What is the area of the white flag?
Show your working.

b What could the **length** and **width** of the white rectangle be?

c Ki is wrong. Explain why.

4 You will need the HMS Rectangle worksheet.
It shows a new flag for the ship.
To complete the flag, we must draw a shaded rectangle inside it.

The **area of the shaded rectangle** must be **20%** of the flag's area.
Draw the rectangle inside the flag.
Use any equipment you think might be helpful.

The SS Triangular

1 30% of this flag is shaded.
What is the **area** of the shaded triangle?
The triangle's height is 45cm.
What is the length of its base?

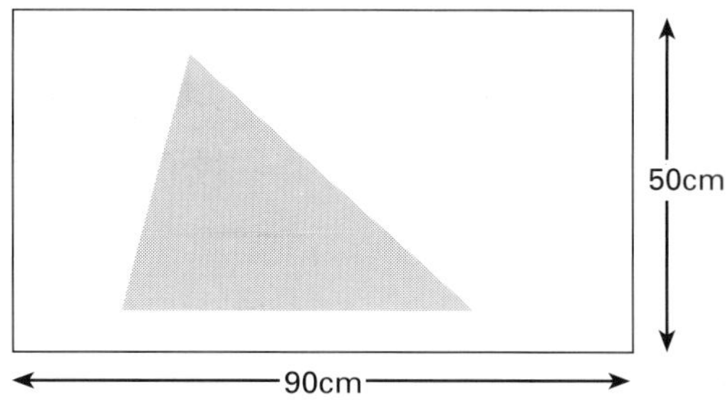

2

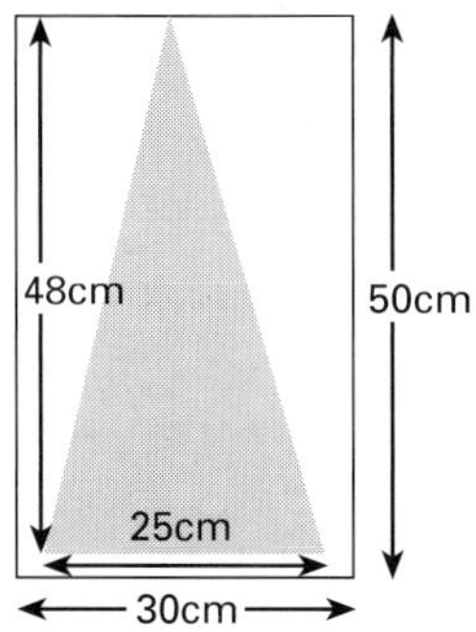

What percentage of this flag is shaded?

3

a 12.5% of this white flag is shaded.
What is the **area** of the white flag?
Show your working.

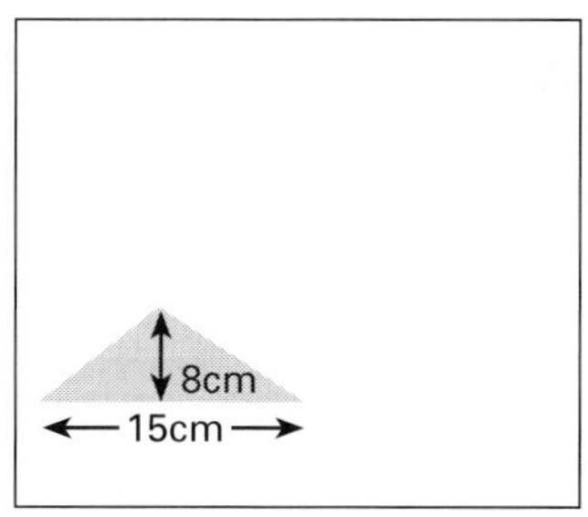

b What could the **length** and **width** of the white rectangle be?

c Ki is wrong. Explain why.

4 You will need the SS Triangular worksheet.
It shows a new flag for the ship.
To complete the flag, we must draw a shaded triangle inside it.

The area of the shaded triangle must be 35% of the flag's area.
Draw the triangle inside the flag.
Use any equipment you think might be helpful.

Problems involving ratio and proportion

A Timetables

Innes High School

1 Here is a timetable for Year 7 pupils at Innes High school.

Mon	Li	Sc	Ma	Ma	LUNCH	Ma	Li		
Tue	Ma	Ma	Li	Sc		Ma	Li		
Wed			Ma	Li		Ma	Ma		Sc
Thur		Li	Ma	Sc		Li	Ma		Ma
Fri	Li	Ma	Ma	Ma		Li	Li		Sc

a Is Neil right? Explain what he means.

b Is Ki right? Explain what she is saying.

c For every **one** Science lesson, how many Maths lessons are there?

d For every **two** Literacy lessons, how many Maths lessons are there?

e What **fraction** of the lessons are Science?

2

Mon					H				
Tue					C				
Wed					N				
Thur					U				
Fri					L				

You will need a timetable worksheet.
You are going to help plan the timetable for Year 8 pupils.

a **One in every five** lessons must be **Maths**.
How many Maths lessons will Year 8 have per week?
Decide when to set Maths lessons on the table.
Mark them on the worksheet with the letters 'MA'.

b **One tenth** of the lessons must be Geography lessons.
Decide when to set Geography lessons on the table.
Mark them on the worksheet with the letters 'GE'.

c For every **two** Geography lessons, there must be **one** RE lesson.
Mark the RE lessons on the timetable.

3

Viv

Can you explain what Viv means?

Stanshall Boys' School

MON	Fr				H					
TUE					C					
WED			Fr		N					
THUR					U					
FRI	Fr				L					

You will need the Stanshall Boys' School timetable worksheet.
You are going to plan the timetable for Year 9 pupils.

1 French lessons are already marked on the table.
The ratio of French to Maths lessons must be 1:3.
How many Maths lessons will Year 9 have per week?
Decide when to set Maths lessons on the table.
Mark them on the worksheet with the letters 'Ma'.

2 **One fifth** of the week's lessons must be English.
Choose when to timetable English lessons and mark them on the timetable with the letters 'Eng'.

3. There will be 10 Science lessons per week.
   Some will be Chemistry, some will be Biology.
   The ratio Chemistry : Biology will be 2:3.

   Mark Chemistry and Biology lessons on the timetable.

4. There are to be 12 Humanities lessons.
   For every one RE lesson, there should be three Geography lessons.
   The ratio of History lessons to RE lessons should be 2:1.

   Decide how many RE, History and Geography lessons to timetable.
   Mark them on the timetable.

5. There should be two Design and Technology lessons per week.
   Is this possible?

6. The School must ensure that 40% of lesson time is given to the **core** subjects – Maths and English. Have they achieved this?
   Explain your reasoning.

Longfellow County School

MON					Lunch			
TUE								
WED								
THUR								
FRI								

You will need the Longfellow County School timetable worksheet. You are going to use the information below to plan the timetable for Year 11 pupils.

- 20% of the lessons must be Science.
- There should be twice as many Design & Technology lessons as Business Studies lessons.
- One seventh of the lessons must be History or Geography.
- The ratio Business Studies : RE should be 1:1.
- There should be one more History lesson than Geography lessons.
- Year 11 should have two RE lessons per week.
- The Science lessons should be split between Biology, Chemistry and Physics in the ratio 2:3:2.
- Two sevenths of the lessons should be split equally between English and Maths.
- The remaining lessons are Modern Foreign Languages.

B Ratio problem bank

1 Ki and Hussein have collected game cards.
Hussein has collected more than Ki.

Which of the friends is right? Explain why.

2 If Ki had 7 cards, how many would Hussein have?
If Hussein had 27 cards, how many would Ki have?
Show your working.

3 In Year 7 at Innes High School,
there are 3 boys for every 4 girls.
There are 27 boys in the Year.
How many girls are there?

4 In Year 8 there are 7 boys for every 6 girls.
There are 36 girls in the Year.
How many boys are there?

5 In Year 9 there are 60 pupils.
There are 2 girls for every 3 boys.
How many girls are there in Year 9?
How many boys?

6 Hussein spent £12 at the bookshop. He bought a magazine and a book. The book cost 3 times as much as the magazine. How much did the book cost?

7 6 bars of chocolate cost £1.26. How much do 4 bars cost?

8 A recipe for tomato soup uses 3 tomatoes for every litre of soup. How many tomatoes do you need to make 2 litres of soup?

9 Chicken must be cooked 50 minutes for every kg.

a How long does it take to cook a 4kg chicken?

b

How many kg does Monica's chicken weigh?

10

YORKSHIRE PUDDING
Ingredients: 50g cheese 100g butter 250g flour

a Monica makes a smaller pudding. She has 40g of butter. How much cheese will she need? How much flour? Show your working.

b Hussein decides to make a 480g pudding. How much flour will he need?

c Monica's pudding needed 3 eggs. How many will Hussein need?

11

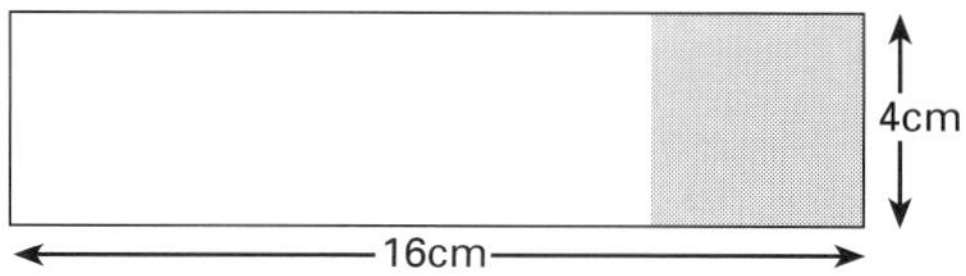

Look at the diagram.
The shaded shape is a square.
Show that the ratio of white : shaded is 3:1.

12 Look at the diagram. The white triangle is an isosceles triangle. What is the ratio of areas, shaded : white?

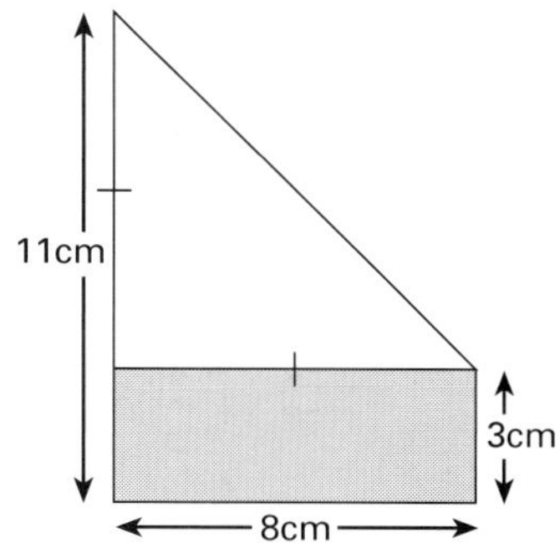

13

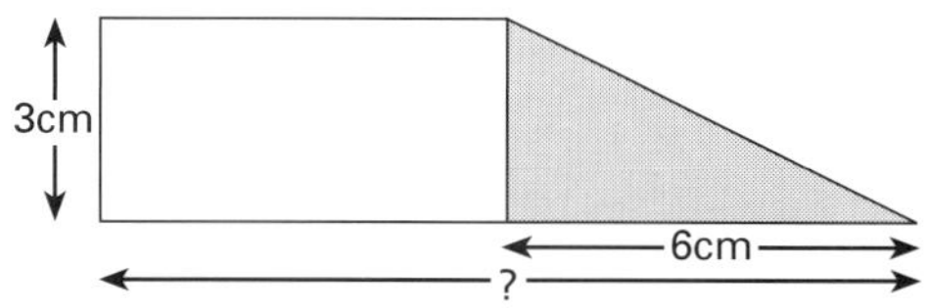

In this diagram, the ratio of white to shaded is 2:1.
Show that the missing length is 12cm.

14 In this diagram, the ratio shaded : white is 2:3.
Work out possible values for the missing dimensions.

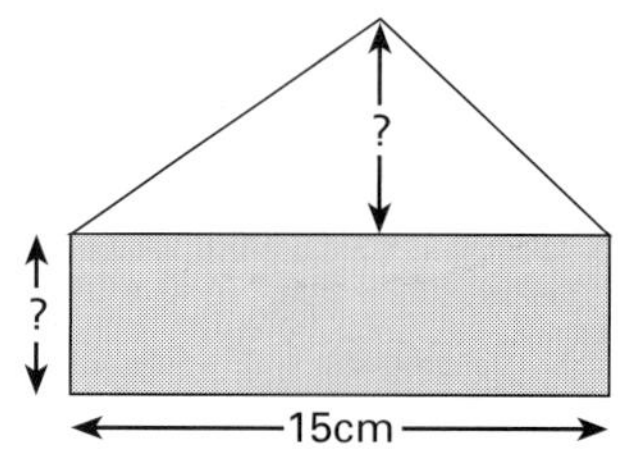

15

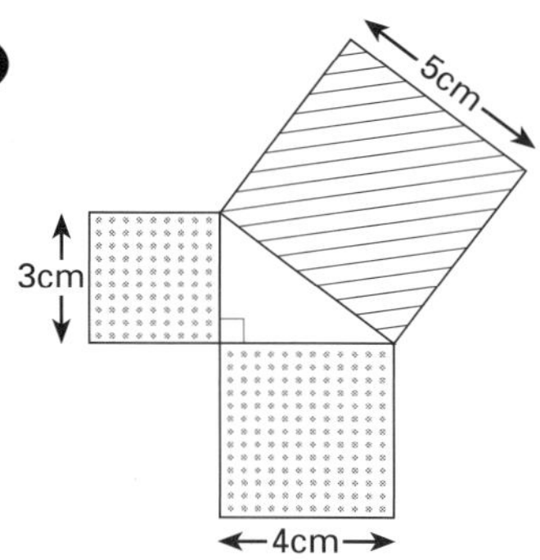

The diagram shows a right-angled triangle with three squares drawn at each side.
Show that the ratio dotted area : striped area is 1:1.

16 Imagine a different right-angled triangle with different side lengths.
Imagine dotted squares and a striped square drawn at each side.
Show that the ratio dotted : striped will still be 1:1.

C Populations

1. How many 1000s are there in 43 million?
How many 500s are there in 28 million?
Show your working.

2. 1 in every 200 people will die this year in the UK from smoking.
The population of the UK is approximately 59 million.
How many people will die this year from smoking?

3.

Country	Births per 1000 of population	Population (Millions)
Afghanistan	42	26
Bolivia	28	8
Turkey	19	65
UK	11	59

Which of the friends is correct?
Show your working.

4 Problems involving number and algebra

A Number cards

700	310	80	4	77	2.5	$x+26$
500	590	50	5	54	8.8	x
400	173	40	8	83	4.5	$64-x$
100	167	10	6	36	4.2	$10-x$

1. Choose **two** cards that add together to make a total of 90. Write the two numbers down.
2. Find as many **pairs** of cards that add to make 90 as you can.
3. **Three** of the cards add together to make 90. Which three cards are they?
4. Find as many sets of **three** cards that sum to a total of 90 as you can.
5. How could we **extend** this puzzle using the cards?
6. Choose a number from the target board below.

600	23	26	-4	72.5
660	495	14	2	45.2
320	396	43	0.3	$x-6$
90	317	-3	4.3	$10-2x$
20	694	-2	0.8	54

The number you have chosen is the **difference** between two of the number cards. Which two cards are they?

7. Choose another number from the target board.
It is the difference between two other number cards.
Which two?
See how many differences from the board you can match to two number cards.

8. Choose two cards and subtract one from the other.
Tell your friend the difference.
Now ask your friend to find the two cards you subtracted.

B Sum puzzles

17 22 58 26 47 13 27 12

1. Look at the list of numbers.
Ki added two of them together.
She wrote her answer down:

■ 4

Which pair of numbers did Ki add together?
Is there more than one answer?
Explain how you spotted pairs that fit.

2. Here are some more sums with a blank in the tens column.
One of the sums **cannot** be made by adding two numbers from the list.
Which one is impossible? Explain your reasoning.

■ 5　　■ 1　　■ 2　　■ 9　　■ 0

3. Use each of the digits 2, 3, 4, 5, 6 and 8 once to make this sum correct:

■ ■ + ■ ■ = ■ ■

Keep a record of the sums you have tried.
Explain how you found a sum that works.
Is there more than one possible answer?

4. Make the sum correct using the digits 1, 2, 4, 6, 7 and 9 once.

5. Use the digits 3, 5, 7 and 9 as many times as you like to make these sums correct:

■■ + ■■ = 114 ■■ + ■■ = 150
■■ + ■■ = 96 ■■ + ■■ = 188
■■ + ■■ = 92 ■■ + ■■ = 110

6. Find **all** the pairs of positive two-digit integers that sum to make 42.

Monica

Which of your pairs has the smallest difference? The largest?
What do you notice?

7. Look at this statement. It shows two positive two-digit numbers that sum to 42.

⊘☺ + 😐☹ = 42

Viv Hussein Ki

Which of the friends is right?
Can you explain why?
Can you complete what Ki is saying?
Can you add to what Viv is saying so that it becomes true?

C Consecutive integers

1 Find three consecutive integers that add together to give a total of 39.
Explain how you found your answer.

2 Find three consecutive integers that sum to make 132.

3 Choose a number from the target board.
Find the three consecutive integers that add to give your chosen number.

4

Neil added his three numbers together to find the total.
Monica did the same with hers.
Can you **predict** the difference between their totals?
Can you explain your prediction?

5 Predict the difference between Viv's total and Hussein's.
Explain your reasoning.

6 Ki has three consecutive number cards.
She is hiding the numbers.
The difference between her total and Viv's is 15.
What are the three consecutive numbers on her cards?
Explain your reasoning.
Is there more than one possible answer?

❼ 

Ki

What do the totals have in common?
Will that be true of the sum of **any** three consecutive integers? Why?

❽ Here are cards for three consecutive integers.
Write expressions for the two blank cards.

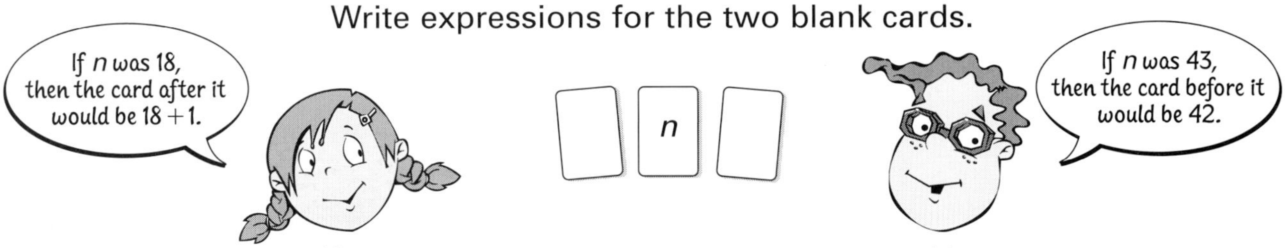

Monica

Viu

❾ Add your three expressions together.
What do you notice?
How could we use this to explain what Ki noticed about the totals in question 7?

❿ A link exists between the product of any **four** consecutive positive integers and **some** of the square numbers. Find the link.

D Shape expressions

1 $2 + 8 = 10$, so...

Which of these statements can we write next to this calculation?

...$10 - 8 = 2$ ...$7 + 1 = 8$ ...$8 + 2 = 10$

...$10 + 2 = 8$ ...$10 - 2 = 8$

2 $5 + 7 = 12$, so...

Write **three** statements that follow from this calculation.

3 $2 \times 14 = 28$, so...

Write three statements that follow from this calculation.

4

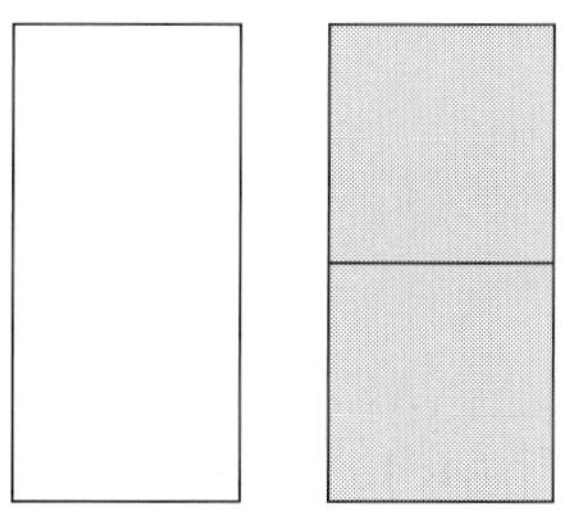

Function cards

$g = w$ $2g = w$ $g = 2w$

$g = \frac{1}{2}w$ $w = 2g$

In this drawing, the grey rectangles are **half** the length of the white rectangle.
Which function cards shows the relation between g and w?

Which of the friends is right? Can you help Neil?
Can you finish what Hussein is saying?

5 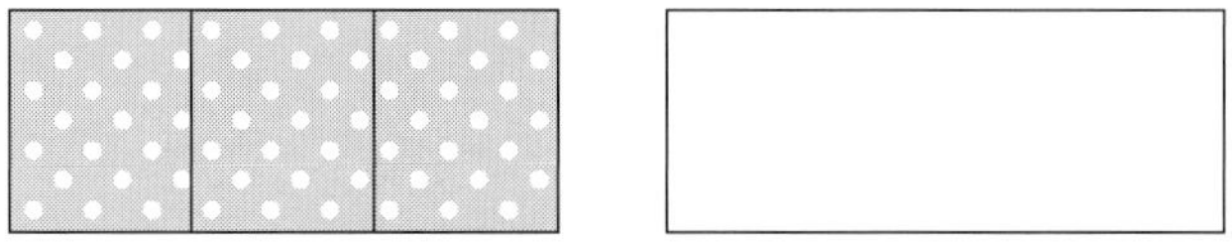

In this diagram, the dotted rectangles are **one third** the length of the white rectangle.
Write a function to show the relation between *d* and *w*.

6 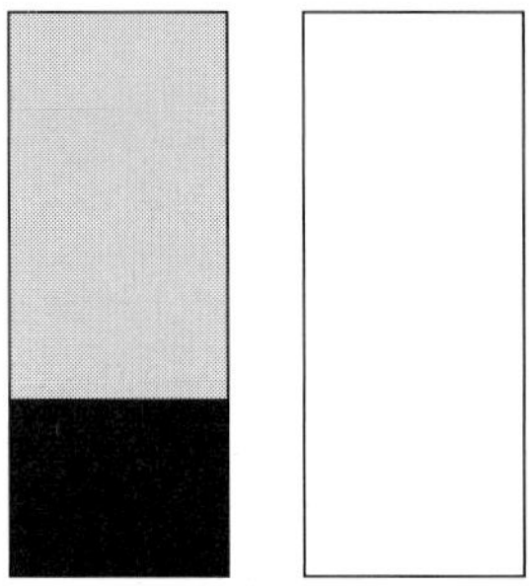

Function cards

$w+b=g$ | $b+g=w$ | $w-b=g$ | $w=g-b$ | $b=w-g$

Look at the diagram. Which function cards describe the relation between *w*, *g* and *b*?

7 Draw a diagram with a white rectangle and some grey and black rectangles to show the relation: $w=g+2b$.

8 In these diagrams, the length of the rectangle is **always** 14cm and the width is **always** 9cm.
For each diagram, find the lengths *a* and *b*.

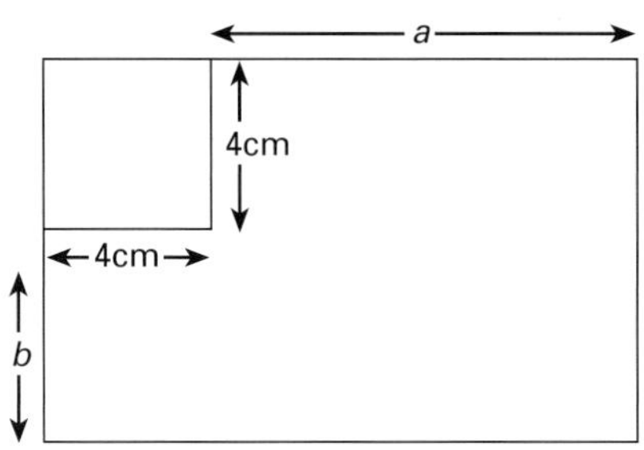

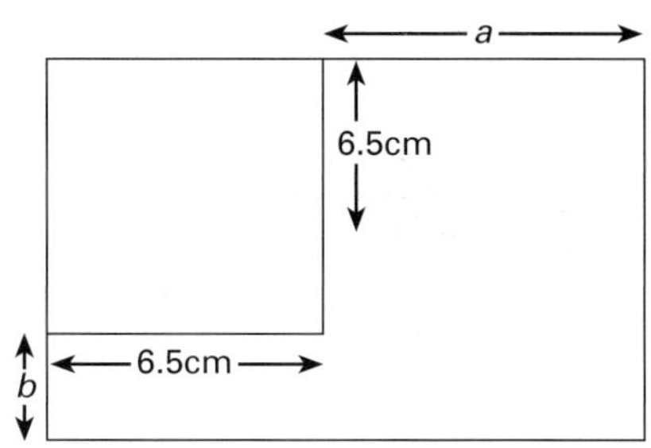

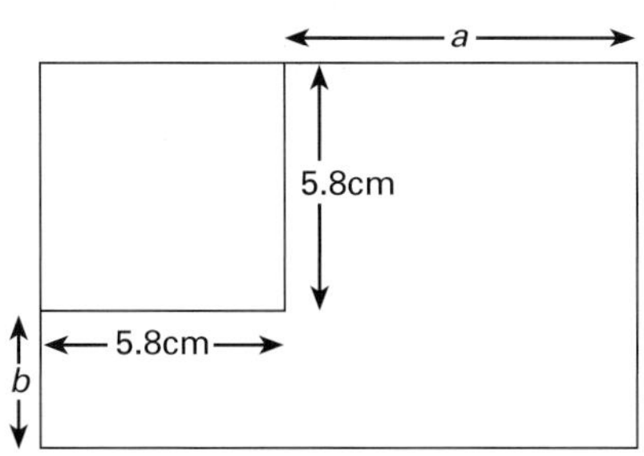

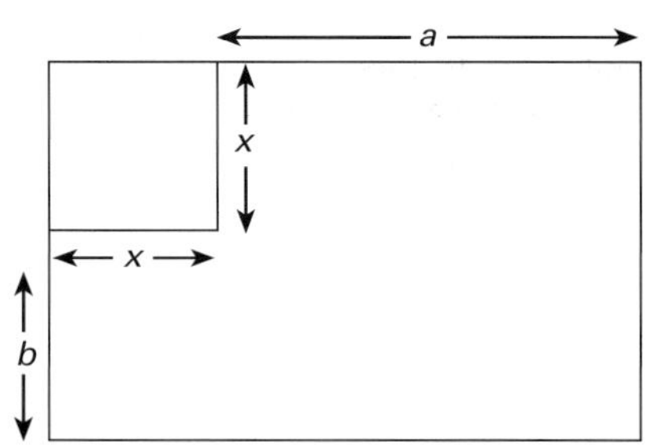

9

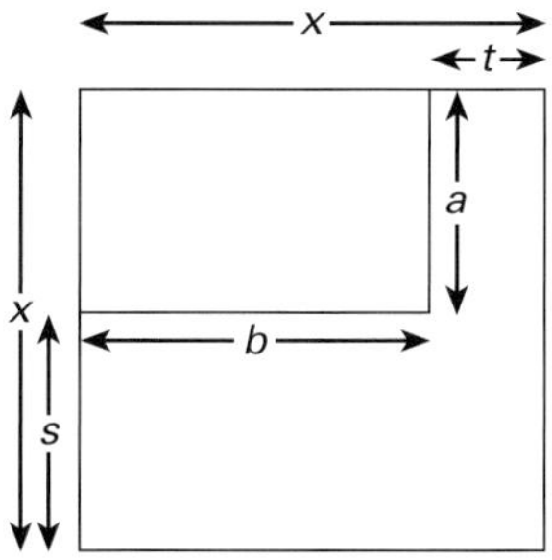

The diagram shows a square.
Which of these function cards is true?

$x = t + b$	$x - t = b$	$s + a = x$
$a - s = b$	$s + a = t + b$	$s + t + a + b = 2x$

10 In this diagram, an isosceles triangle with equal sides (t) has been drawn inside a rectangle of length a and width b. Write as many function statements as you can to describe the relations in the diagram.

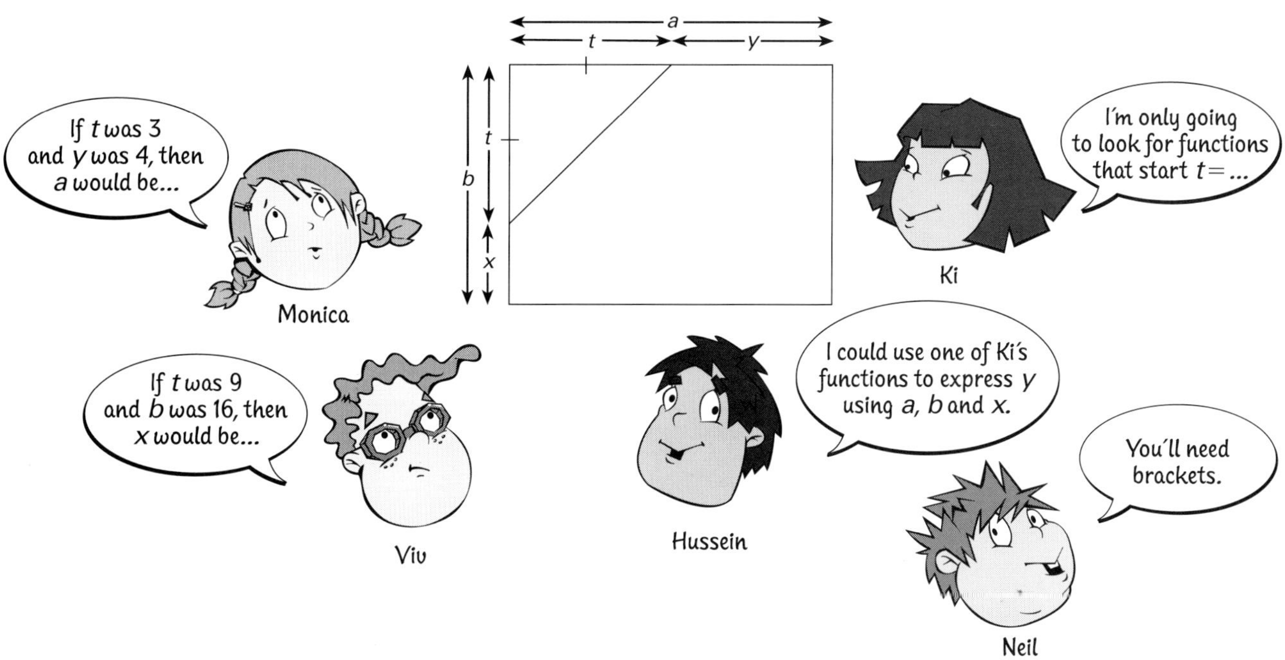

11

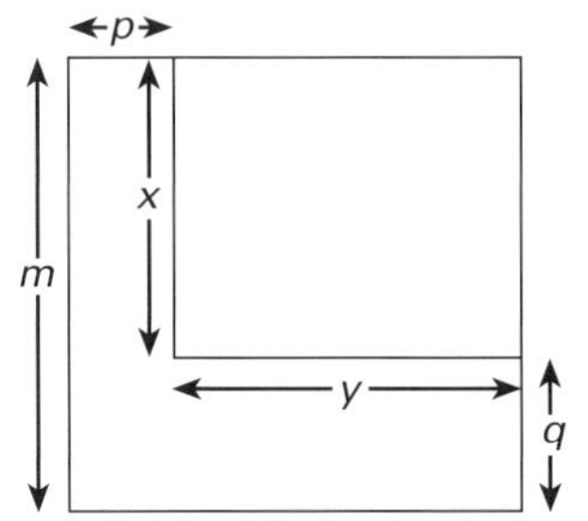

This square has sides of length m.

Express:

a q in terms of m and x.

b m in terms of y and p.

Now express q in terms of p, y and x.

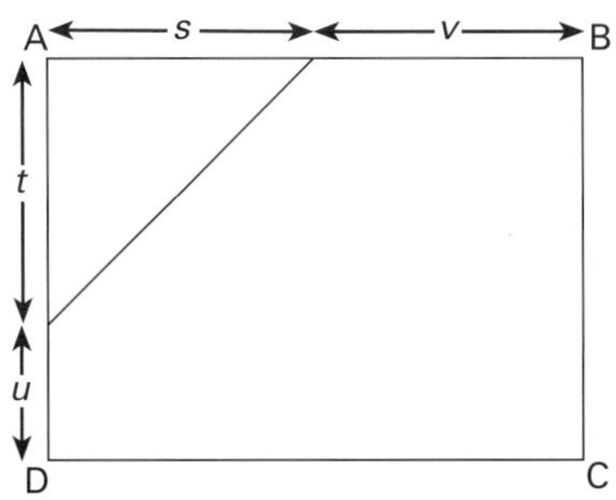

12 Express the perimeter of rectangle ABCD in terms of s, t, u and v.

13 Express the area of rectangle ABCD in terms of s, t, u and v.

14 Triangle DEF is an equilateral triangle with side length t cm.
Arcs with centres D, E and F are drawn as shown.

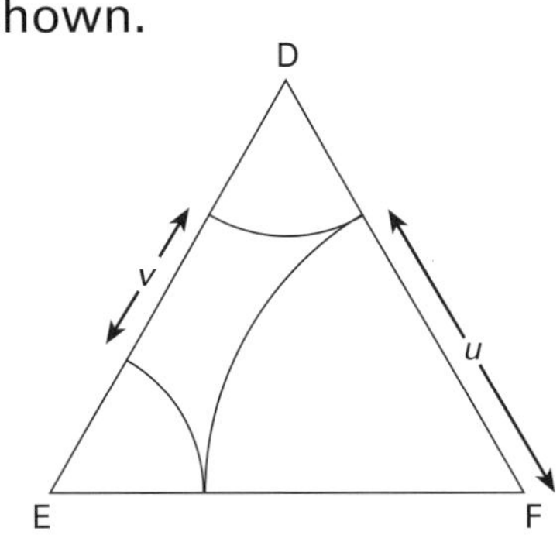

Express v in terms of t and u.

15

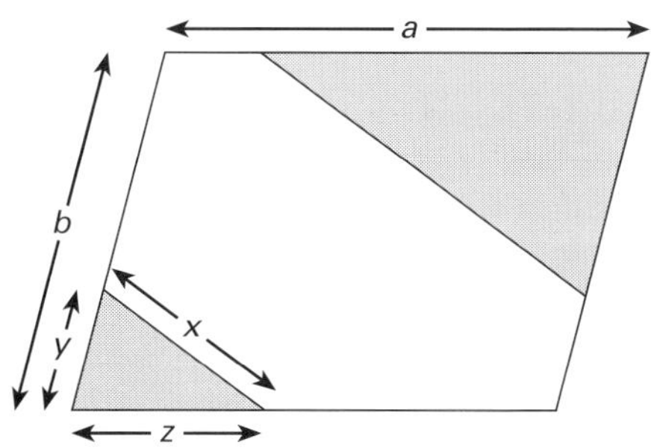

The diagram shows a parallelogram, with sides a and b.
A triangle with sides x, y and z is drawn as shown.
The second shaded triangle shown is an enlargement of the first, scale factor 2.
Find an expression for the perimeter of the shaded hexagon.

16

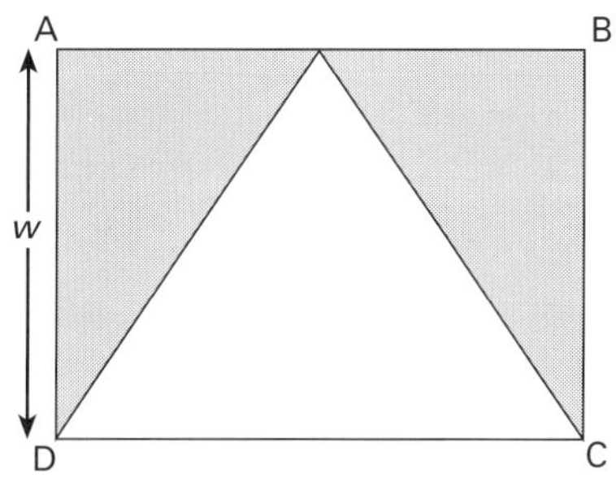

The length of rectangle ABCD is twice its width.
Write an expression for the combined area of the two shaded regions in terms of the rectangle's width.

17

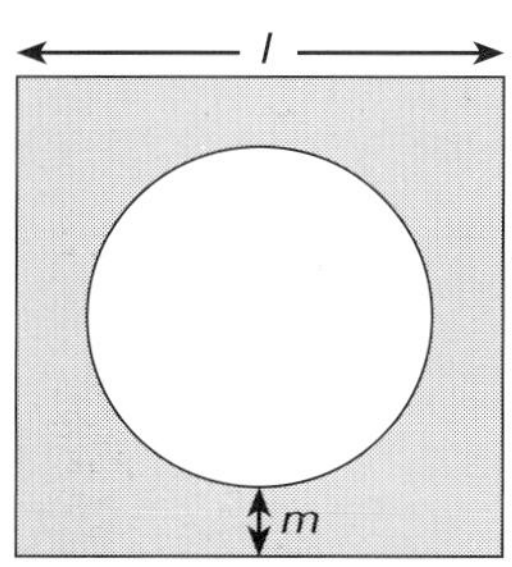

The diagram shows a circle drawn inside a square, side length l cm. The centre of the circle coincides with the centre of the square.
Derive an expression for the area of the shaded region outside the circle.

5 Problems to solve with a graphical calculator

A Investigate the calculator: sequences

1. Type the keys [2] [ENTER]
   Then [ANS] [+] [2] [ENTER]
   Then [ENTER] [ENTER]
   [ENTER] [ENTER]

   Write a sentence to explain the numbers that the calculator displays. How many times must you press [ENTER] before you reach the number 78?

2. Look at the keys you pressed in problem 1. Which keys should we press to get the **odd** numbers starting with 1? Which keys should you press to get the **multiples of 3** starting with 3?

3. Imagine typing the keys [7] [ENTER]
   Then [ANS] [+] [7] [ENTER]
   Then [ENTER] [ENTER] [ENTER] [ENTER]

   Write down the numbers you would see on the display.

4. Imagine typing the keys [3] [ENTER]
   Then [ANS] [+] [5] [ENTER]
   Then [ENTER] [ENTER] [ENTER] [ENTER]

   Write down the numbers you would see on the display.
   Now type the keys to check your numbers.

5. Ki typed some keys and the display showed these numbers:

Ki

   Write down the keys that Ki typed to make this sequence.

6 Which keys would we type to display this sequence?

```
200
100
 50
 25
12.5
```

What are the next four terms in this sequence?

7 Generate these sequences on your calculator:

a 4, 7, 10, 13...
b 9, 16, 23, 30...
c 1, 5, 25, 125...
d 256, 128, 64, 32...
e 2, -4, 8, -16, 32...

Write down the keys you typed for each sequence.

8 Imagine typing the keys [3] [ENTER]
Then [(] [ANS] [*] [3] [)] [−] [2] [ENTER]

Explain why the second term in this sequence will be 7.
Predict the next four terms.
Now type the keys and check your sequence.

9 Hussein typed some keys and the display showed this sequence:

```
  2
  5
 14
 41
122
```

Hussein

Write down the keys that Hussein typed to generate this sequence.

10 Here are the first two terms of a sequence:

4, 7…

Viv, Monica and Neil used their graphical calculators to generate a sequence that began 4, 7…

Viv

Monica

Neil

Investigate with your calculator to find the rules which they used to generate three **different** sequences.

11 Investigate with your calculator to see how many different sequences you can generate that begin:
8, 3…
Write down the rules that you use.

Open the TABLE display on your calculator.
Look at the line Y1 =
Type the keys: [2] [.] [3] [X,θ,T] [ENTER]
Now press TABLE.

12 Describe the numbers in the two columns of the table you can see.
Complete the two statements:

The Y numbers are the X numbers multiplied by ☐.

The ☐ numbers are the c numbers divided by ☐.

13 What is 2.3×7?

14 Find the product of 19 and 2.3.

15 What is 36.8 ÷ by 2.3?

16 Write down the products of 2.3 and **15** and 2.3 and **12**. Use your two answers to show that the product of 2.3 and **27** is 62.1.

17 What number is halfway between 2.3×7 and 2.3×11?

18 Move the cursor using the arrow keys to the Y1 column heading.
Press ENTER

You can now change the relationship between the X numbers and Y numbers.

Type 1 7 X,θ,T ENTER

What is 102 ÷ 17?

19 Hussein typed in a new formula relating X and Y. Here is a part of the table he made:

X	Y1		
4	30		
5	37.5		
6	45		
7	52.5		

Complete the keys that Hussein typed into the Y1 line:
Y1 = ☐ ☐ ☐ X

20 Look at the following calculations:
28.5 ÷ 3 =
180.5 ÷ 9.5 =
23 × 9.5 =

Type in a new formula on the calculator to find the answers to these calculations.

B Draw shapes

1 Choose the LINE instruction on your graphical calculator.

When you see the word **Line** on your screen, type:

(1 , 1 , 1 , 4) ENTER

Write a sentence to describe the line you have drawn.
What are the co-ordinates of the two end-points of your line?
What do you notice?

2 Viv tried to draw the line for question 1. This is what he typed:

Viv

```
Line (1, 1, 14)
```

When he pressed ENTER, the calculator showed this message:

```
ERR:ARGUMENT
1: Quit
2: Goto
```

What mistake did Viv make?

3. What instructions should you type to draw a line with end points at (2, 1) and (2, 5)? Will the new line be parallel to the first line?

   Use the calculator to draw the line. Was your prediction correct?

4. Use the calculator to draw a line connecting the points (1, 1) and (2, 1).

5. If we draw a line connecting the two points (1, 4) and (2, 5), what shape will we have drawn?

   Use the calculator to draw the line.

6. Clear the drawing and line numbers you have put in. Use the calculator to draw a rectangle which has vertices at: (1, 1), (1, 3) and (4, 3).

   What will the co-ordinate of the fourth vertex be?

7. Clear your last drawing. Draw a line connecting the points (2, 1) and (6, 1). This line is the base of an isosceles triangle which has a height of 3 units. What are the co-ordinates of the third vertex? Complete the drawing of the triangle.

8. Use the calculator to draw a rectangle. One of the vertices must be at (2, 1). The rectangle must have an area of 12 square units. Is there more than one possible rectangle? How many rectangles could we draw from these instructions?

9 Use the calculator to draw a rectangle with a perimeter of 14 units.

10 Imagine the point (3, 5). This is the top vertex of a new isosceles triangle.
The triangle has a height of 4 units and an area of 4 units squared.
How long must the base be?
Complete a drawing of the triangle.

11 Use the calculator to draw these shapes:

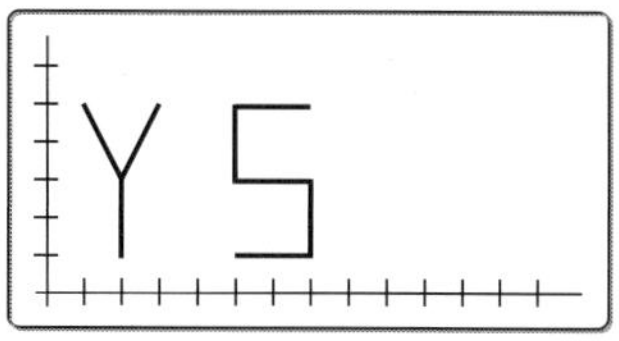

12 Use the calculator to draw this hexagon:

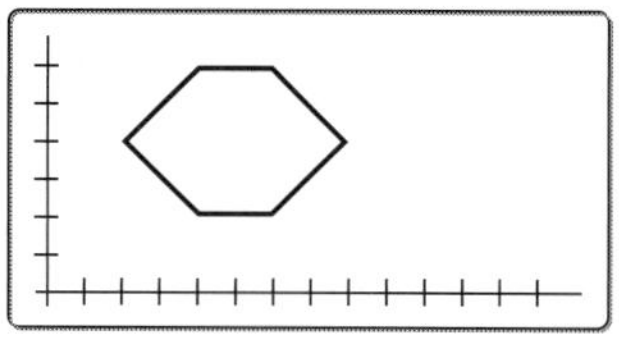

Problems involving shape and space 6

A Dominoes, Quadrominoes, Pentominoes

Dominoes

You will need the Dominoes worksheet.

1. Look at domino 1. Draw a new domino edge-to-edge with domino 1 to make a shape. The shape **must** have **two** lines of symmetry. What order of rotational symmetry does your shape have?

2. Draw a new domino edge-to-edge with domino 2. The shape must have rotational symmetry order 2, but no reflective symmetry.

3. Draw a new domino edge-to-edge with domino 3. The shape must have rotational symmetry order 4 and 4 lines of symmetry.

4. Draw a new domino edge-to-edge with domino 4. The shape must have **no** symmetry at all.

Quadrominoes

You will need squared paper.

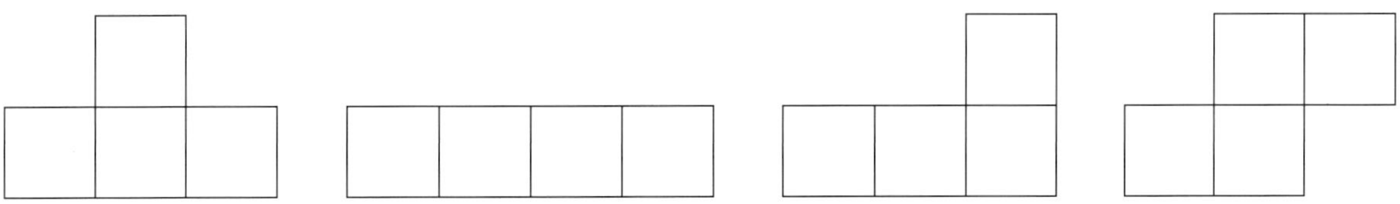

A quadromino is any shape made by joining four squares edge-to edge. Here is an L-shaped quadromino:

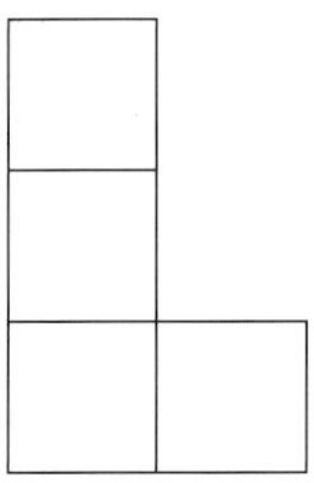

You are going to draw shapes made by joining two L-shaped quadrominoes edge-to-edge.

❶ Draw a shape with no symmetry at all.

❷ Draw a shape with one line of symmetry.

❸ How many **different** shapes can you make with one line of symmetry?

❹ Draw two shapes with rotational symmetry order 2.

Who is right? Investigate.

Pentominoes

A pentomino is any shape made by joining five squares edge-to-edge.
Two different pentominoes are shown:

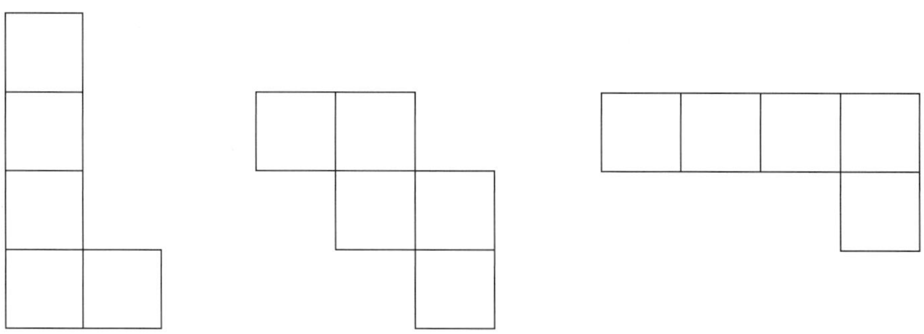

The third shape does not count as a new pentomino. Why not?

1. How many **different** pentominoes can be made by joining five squares in this way? You should make sure that you find **all** possible pentominoes and do not repeat any. How can you make sure?

   Two congruent pentominoes can be joined to make shapes.

2. Read the statements:

   *Some pentominoes **cannot** be joined with another congruent pentomino to make a shape with one line of symmetry.*

   It is impossible to make a shape with rotational symmetry order 4 using 2 pentominoes.

   *Some pentominoes tessellate. Some quadrominoes tessellate. **All** triominoes tessellate.*

   You can make shapes with rotational symmetry order 2 with any 'omino' – domino, triomino, quadromino, pentomino, hexomino, heptomino... whatever.

   Which statements are true?
   If a statement is untrue, explain why.

B Shape and space problem bank

1 Two diagonals have been drawn in this pentagon. Count all the triangles in the pentagon.

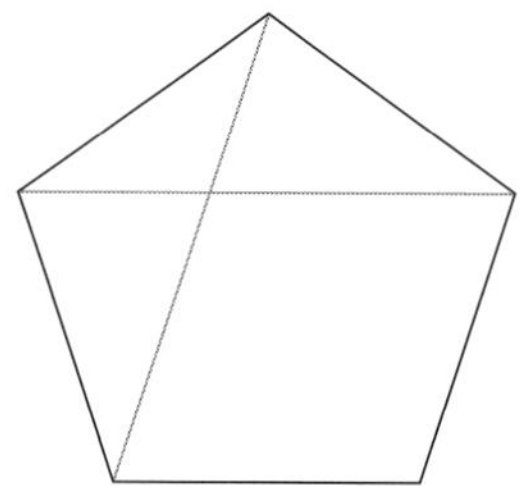

A third diagonal is added. Predict how many new triangles can be counted. Test your prediction.

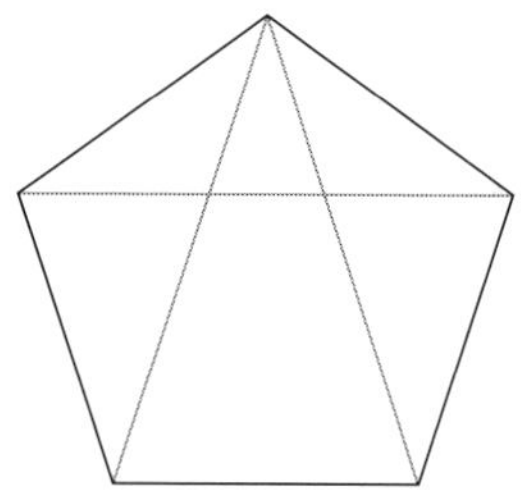

How could this problem be extended?

2 This diagram shows one half of a shape.

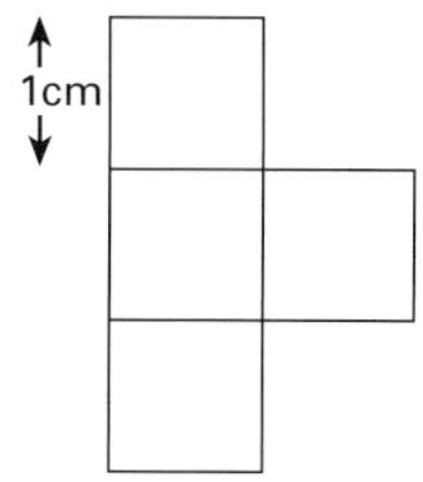

The friends were asked to sketch the whole shape that the original could have been.

Can you sketch the shapes they have drawn? Explain how you drew them.

3 Here are eight diagrams. Each diagram is made by joining two angles together. Sort the diagrams into **two** different groups.

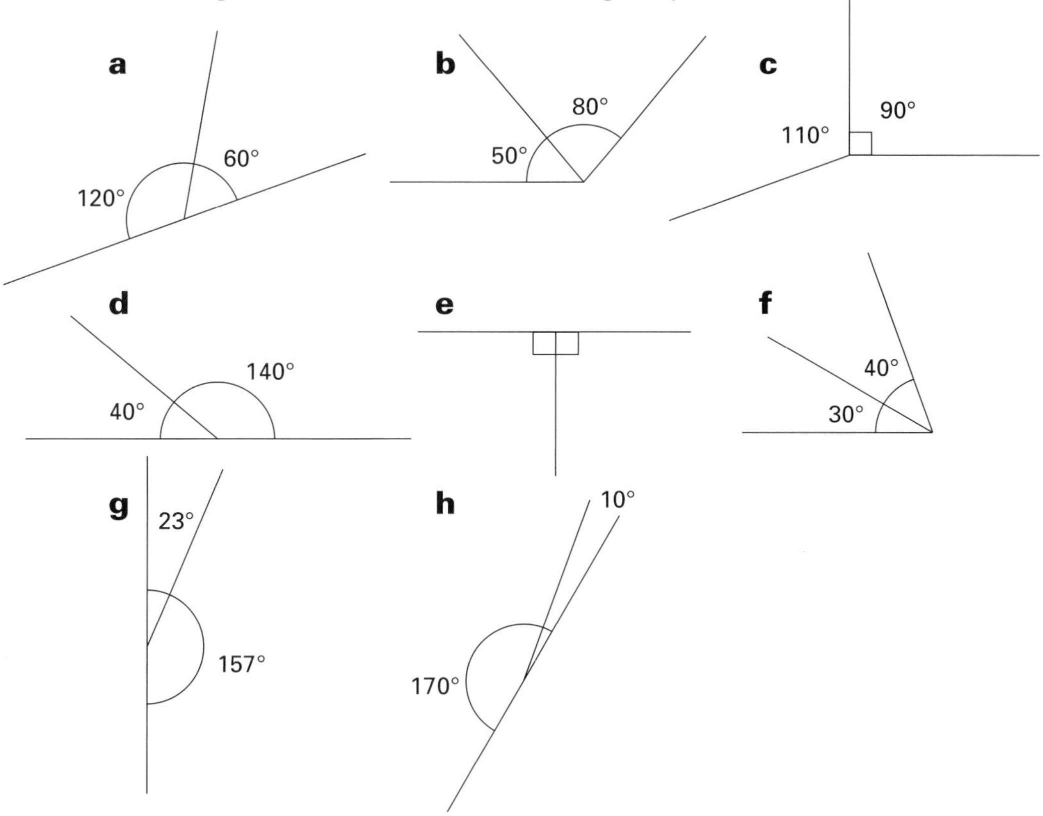

Explain how you sorted the diagrams.
Give each of your groups a name.
What is special about the diagrams in **one** of your groups?

4 Look at the diagram.
Calculate the size of angle *p*.
Show your working.
Do **not** use a protractor (angle measurer).

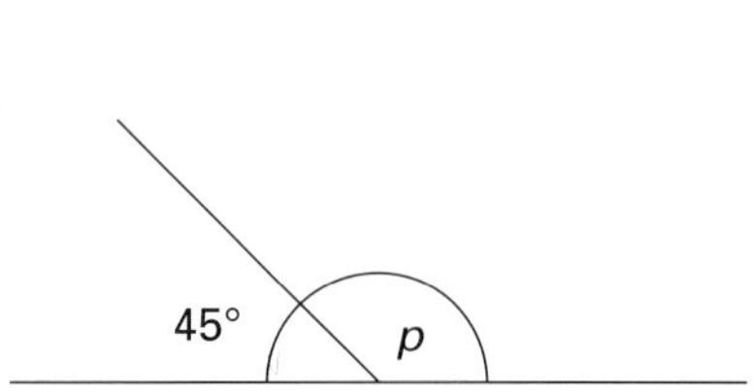

5 Look at the diagram.

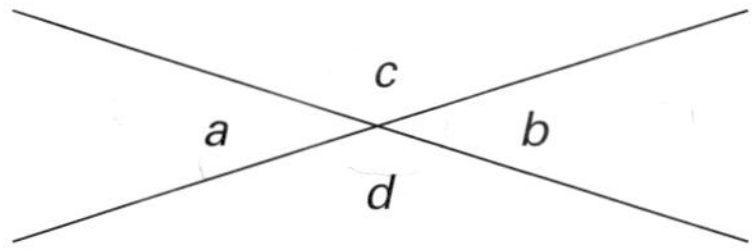

a Which of the angles are equal?
Which angle fact did you use?

b Angle *a* is 35°.
Calculate the size of angles *b*, *c* and *d*.
Do not use a protractor.

6 Here are five quadrilaterals.

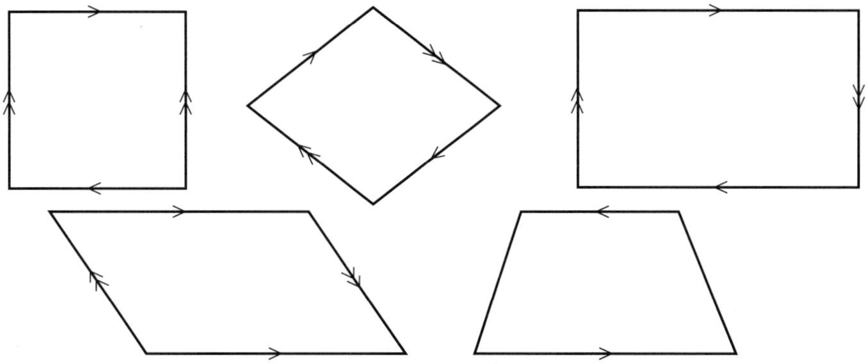

Write a sentence to explain how the trapezium is different to all the other quadrilaterals.

7 Which two lines are parallel?

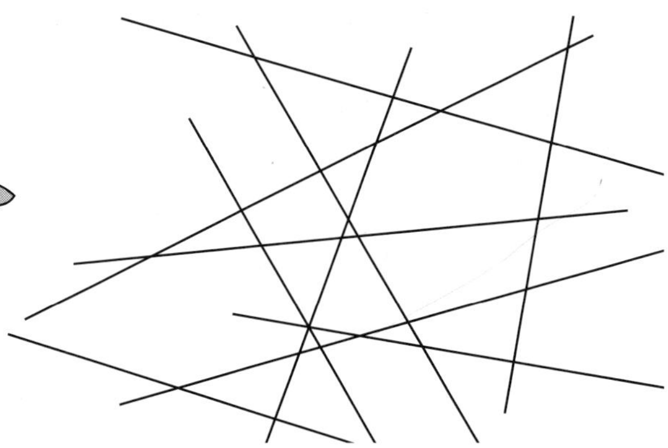

8 Look at the triangle.
Which two angles are equal?

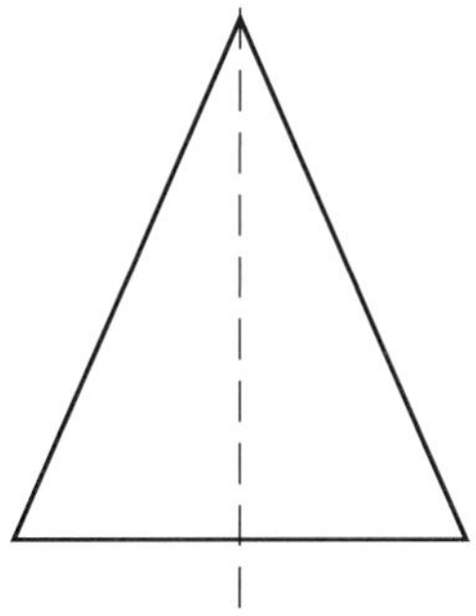

9 Which of these sentences explains what is special about lines which are **perpendicular**?

They are lines of equal length.	*They are lines which join to form an acute angle.*	*They are lines which meet or cross at right angles.*

10 Write a sentence to explain what is special about lines which are **parallel**.

11

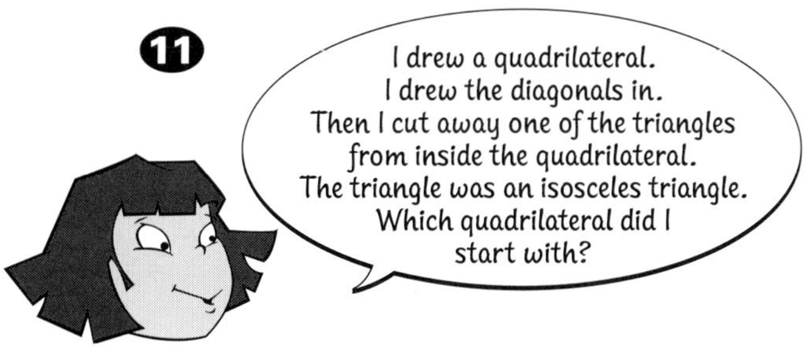

Which quadrilateral did Ki start with?

12 Here is the net of a die. When the net is folded up, the opposite faces of the die must add up to 7. Decide where to write the numbers 3, 4, 5 and 6 on the net.

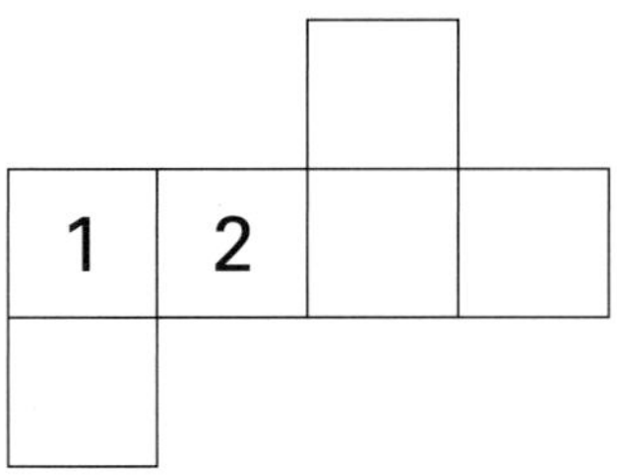

13 Sketch the net of a new die.
Write six consecutive integers onto your net so that, when it's folded up, the opposite faces add to 11.

14 Write a definition of a regular polygon.

15 Imagine a square. Imagine marking the mid-points of each side.
Imagine joining each mid-point.
What is the shape formed inside the square?

16 Test the prediction you made in question 13.
How could we extend this problem?
What shape could we investigate next?

17 Here are the instructions for changing a square, side length 4cm, into a right-angled triangle with lengths 4cm, 3cm and 5cm:

*'From the top left vertex, measure 1cm towards the bottom left vertex and mark a point.
Join that point to the bottom right vertex with a straight line. Now cut along that line.'*

Demonstrate that the instructions are accurate.

18 Write instructions for changing a rectangle, sides 8cm and 18cm, into a trapezium, sides 18cm, 8cm, 12cm and 10cm.

19 Look at the pattern made up of seven circles. If you join three points of intersection, you can draw triangles. Which special types of triangles can you draw?

20

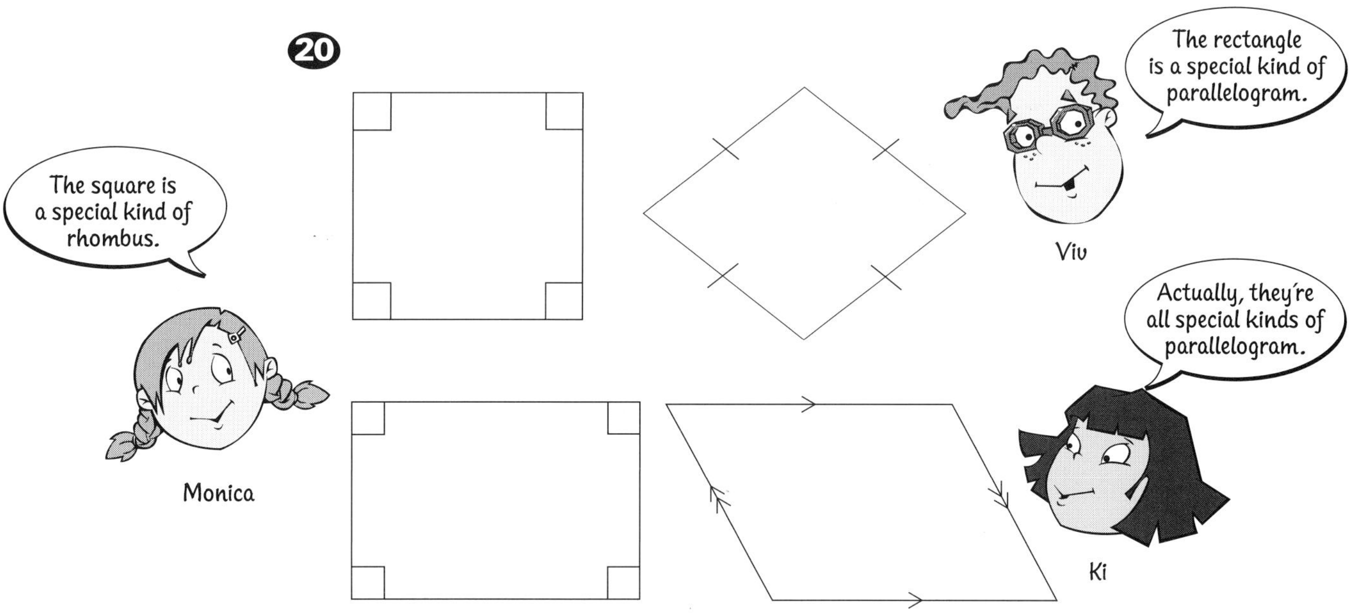

Each of the friends is right.
Explain each of their statements.

21 Explain why a triangle can never have a reflex angle, but a quadrilateral can.

22 The triangle XYZ is isosceles.
Calculate the size of the angles marked q.

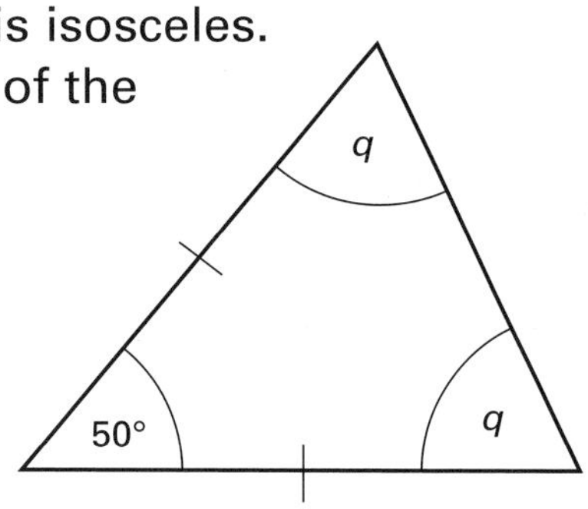

23 Ten identical isosceles triangles are arranged in a pattern.
Calculate the size of angle z.
Show your working.

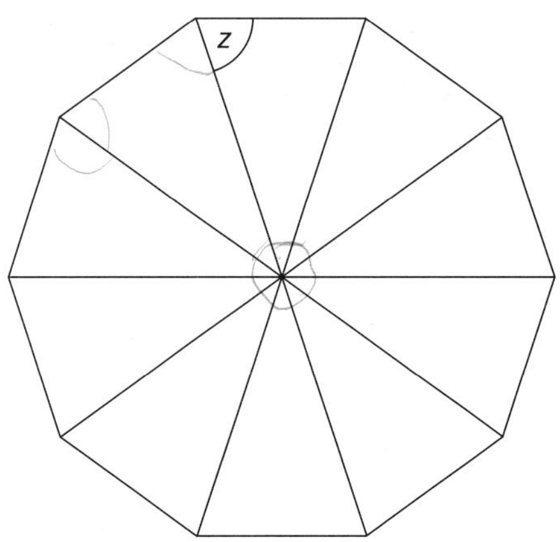

24 Look at the diagram. Exlain why angle *a* must equal 60°. Show your working.

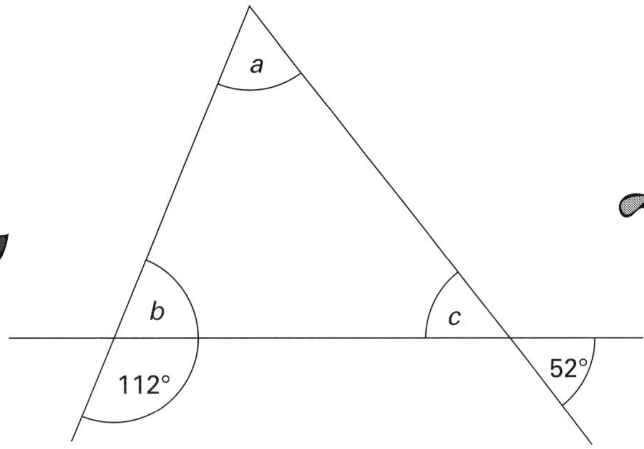

25 What special kind of triangle is triangle DEF?
Explain how you know.
Show all your working.

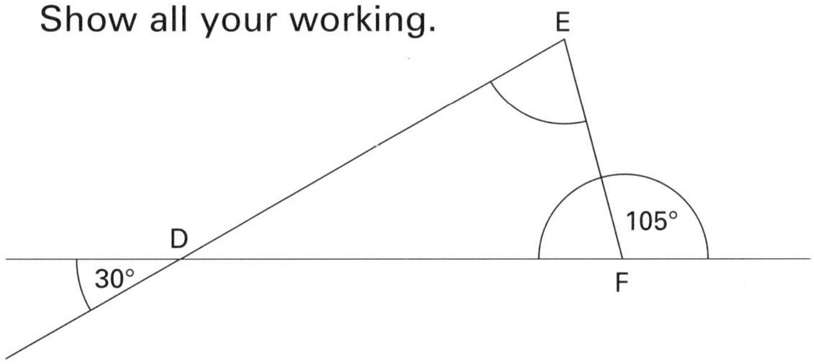

26 This shape is made from a square and two equilateral triangles.

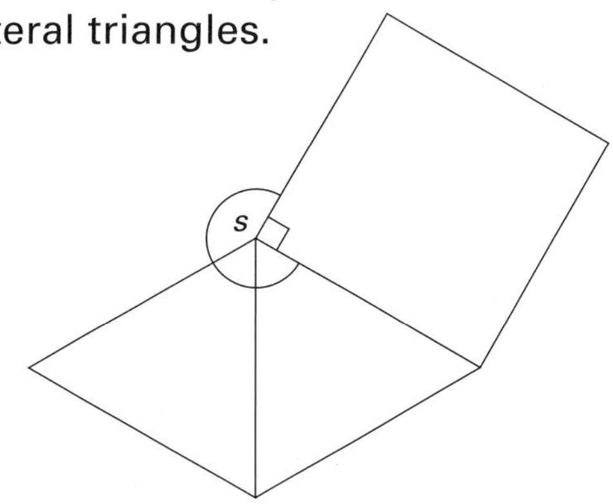

Calculate the size of angle *s*.
Show your method.

27 This shape is made from two congruent isosceles triangles and one square.

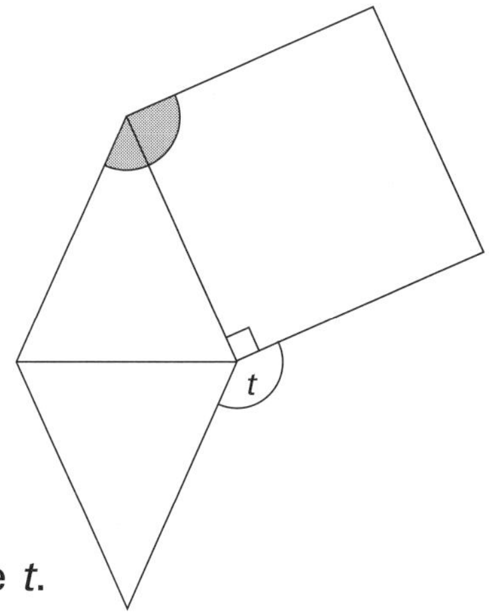

The shaded angle is 130°.
Calculate the size of angle *t*.
Show your method.

28 Calculate the size of angles *u* and *v*.
Show all your working.

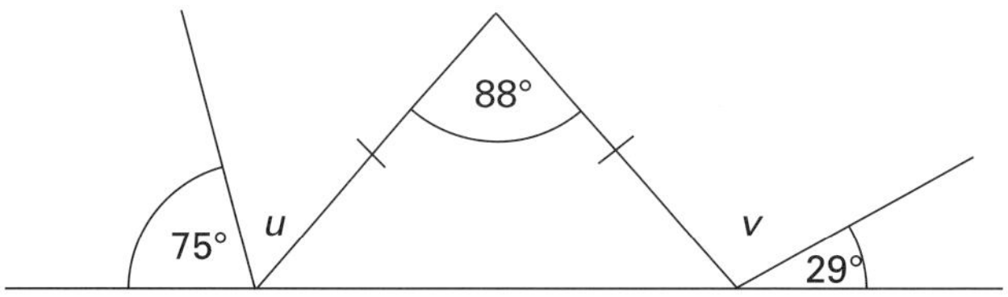

29 'It is a given fact that the interior angle sum for any triangle is 180°.'
What do you think this statement means?

30 The diagram shows a triangle drawn on a straight line.

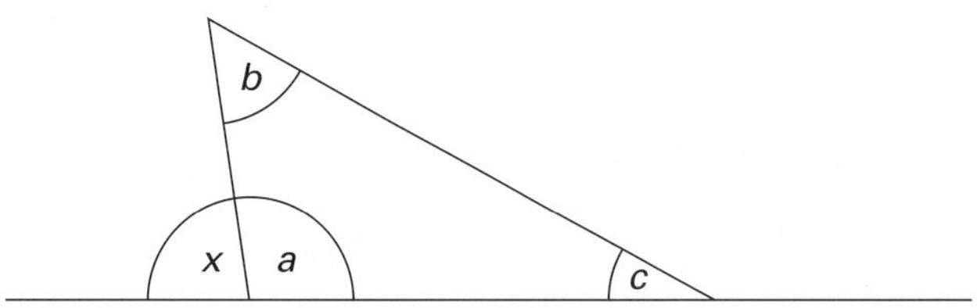

a Write *a* in terms of *x*.
b Write *a* in terms of *c* and *b*.
c Show that $x = b + c$.

31 The diagram shows a quadrilateral.
One diagonal has been drawn.

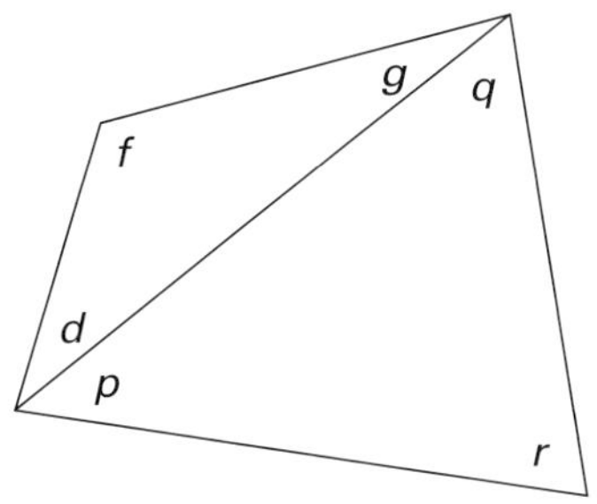

Show that $d + f + g + p + q + r = 360°$.

32 The diagram shows a pentagon.
Two diagonals have been drawn.

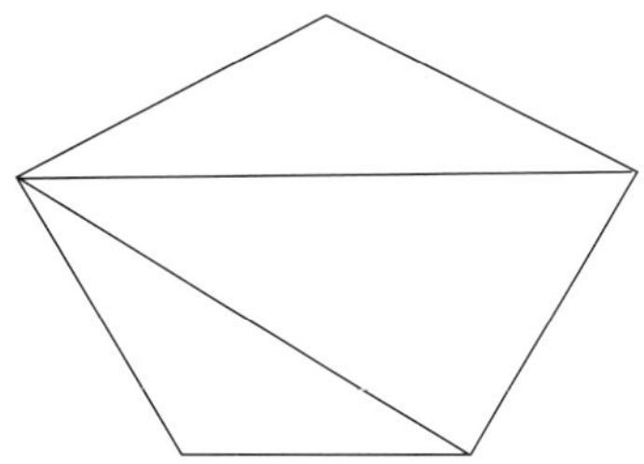

a Find the sum of the five interior angles.

b Show, by using letters for the angles, that your answer to **a** will be true for **any** pentagon and not just this one.

33 Find the interior angle sum for any hexagon.
Prove your result.

7 Problems involving perimeter and area

A Congruent shapes

1. Look at the diagram. It is a grey shape made up of 7 congruent triangles.

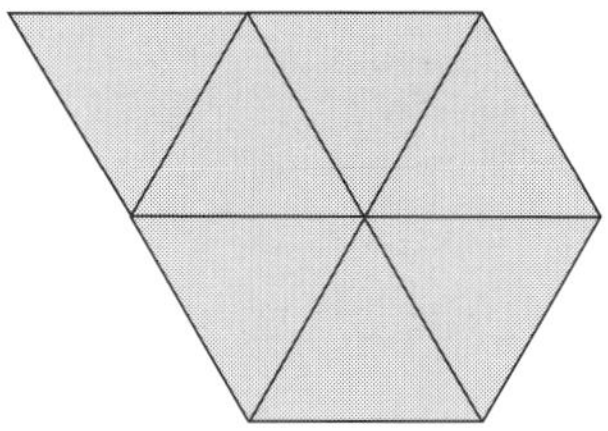

The area of the shape is 42cm^2.
Work out the area of one of the triangles.
Show your working out.

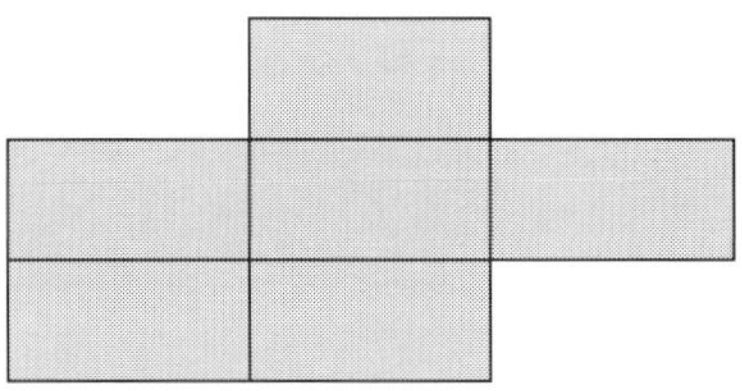

2. Look at the diagram. Write a sentence to describe the grey shape.

3. The area of the shape is 48cm^2.
Work out the area of one of the congruent rectangles.
Show your working out.

4. The length of one of the rectangles is 4cm.

Is Viv correct?
Write a sentence to explain how you know.

5

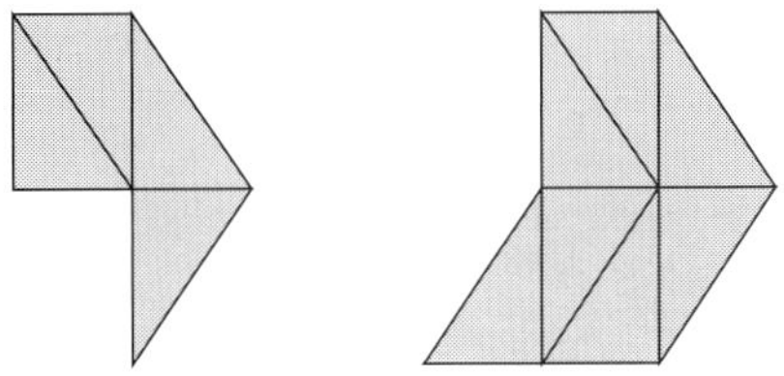

The two shapes are made up of congruent triangles.
The area of the first shape is $36cm^2$.
Find the area of the second shape.
Show your working out.

6

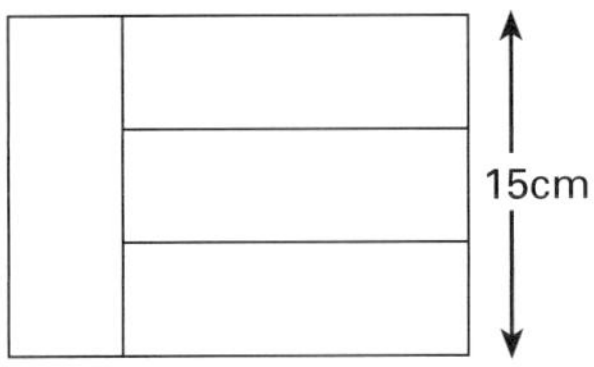

Look at the diagram. Work out the area of one of the congruent rectangles.
Show all your working out.

What is the perimeter of the shape?

7

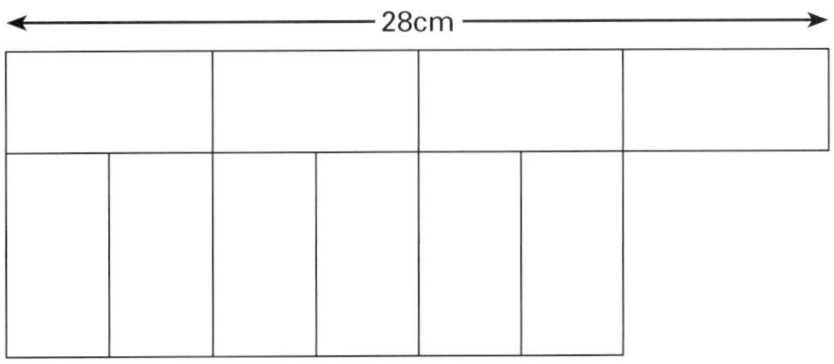

Work out the area of one of the congruent rectangles in this shape.

Work out the perimeter of the shape.
Show all your working out.

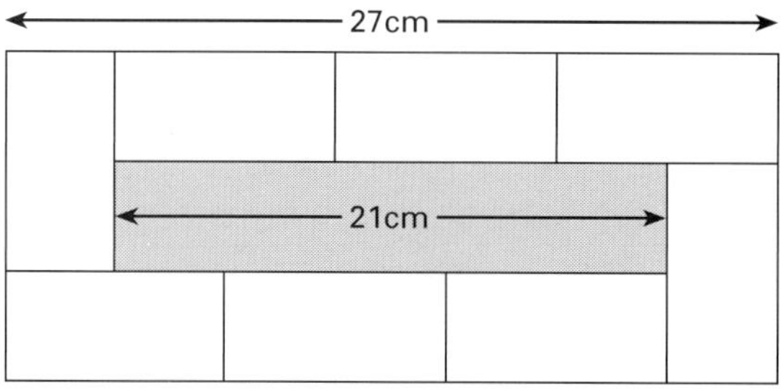

8 Calculate the area of one of the congruent rectangles in this diagram.

9 Calculate the perimeter of the shape.

10 Explain why the grey area inside the shape must be $105cm^2$.

This shape is made of two congruent rectangles and two congruent triangles.

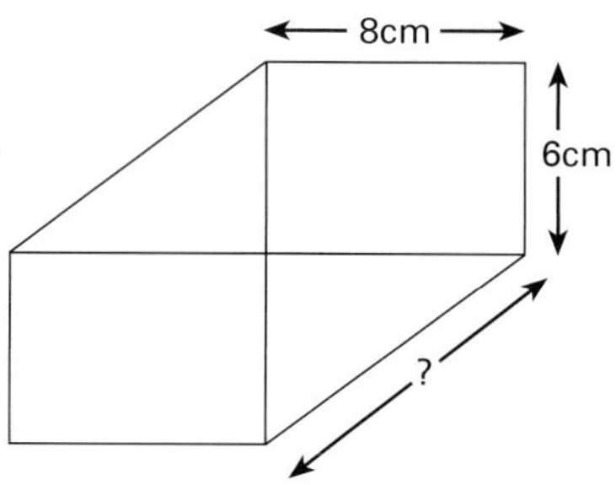

11 What is the area of the shape?

12 The perimeter of the shape is 48cm. What is the longest side of each triangle?

This shape is made of a square and two congruent equilateral triangles.

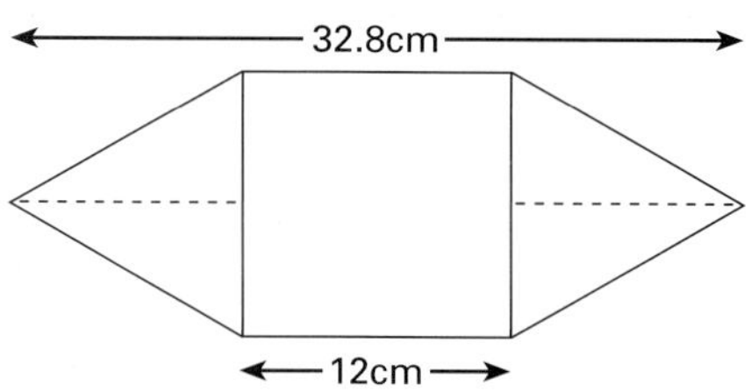

13 Find the perimeter of the shape.

14 Calculate the area of the shape. Show all your working out.

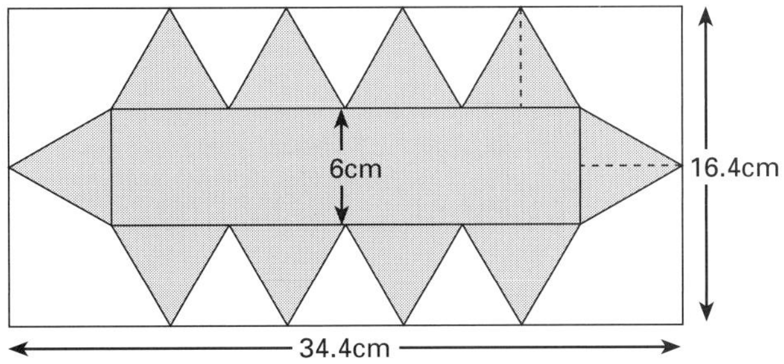

The grey shape is made up of a rectangle and 10 congruent equilateral triangles.
It fits exactly into a larger rectangle.
Neil and Hussein decided to investigate the shape and see how many perimeters and areas they could work out.

15 Choose at least four perimeters or areas from the target board and work them out.
Write down the steps you took to work out your answer.

Perimeter of the large rectangle.	Area of the small rectangle.	Area of the grey shape.	Area of the large rectangle.	Perimeter of the grey shape.
Height of one triangle.	Perimeter of one triangle.	Perimeter of the small rectangle.	Base of one triangle.	Area of one equilateral triangle.

16 Which areas or perimeters were easy to work out straight away?
Which were you not able to work out until you had worked out the easy ones first?

17 How could we extend the investigation?

Triangles like this one:

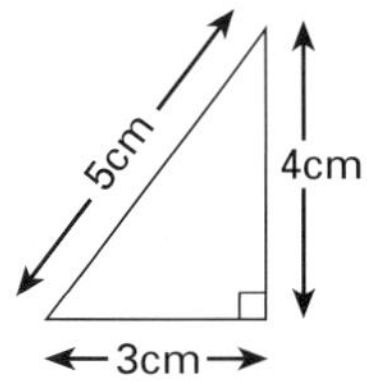

were used to make the shapes in this target board.

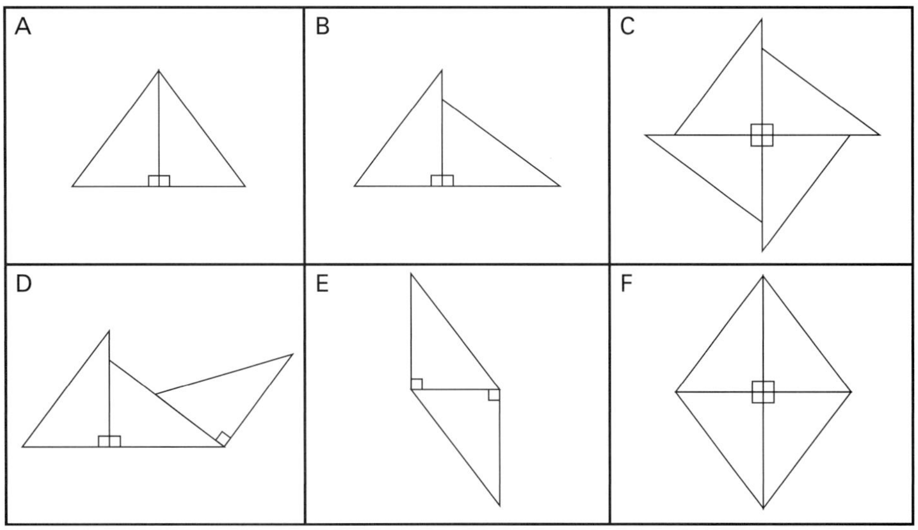

18 Which shapes will have the same area? Explain why.

19 Choose three shapes from the target board. Calculate the area of the shape. Calculate the perimeter of the shape. Show all your working.

Triangles like this one:

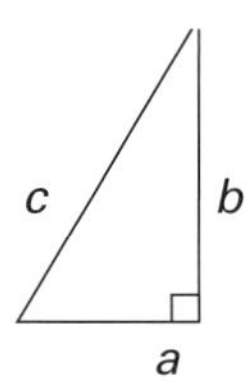

were used to make these shapes:

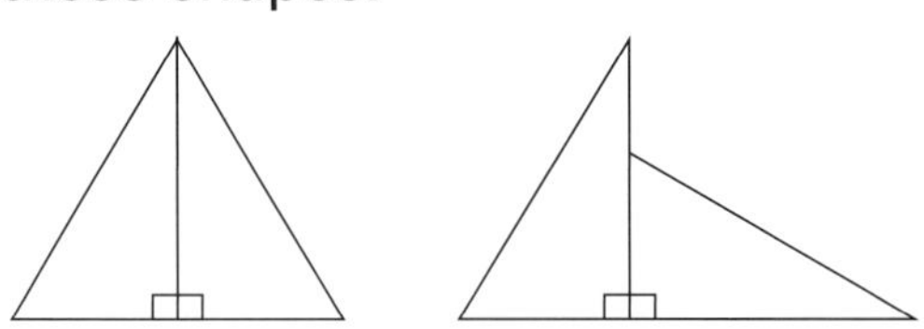

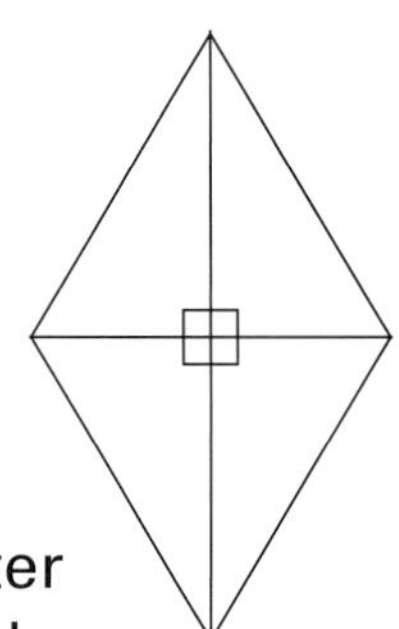

20 Write expressions for the perimeter of each shape in terms of a, b and c.

21 Write expressions for the area of each shape in terms of *a* and *b*.

22 Find the area of the rhombus PQRS.

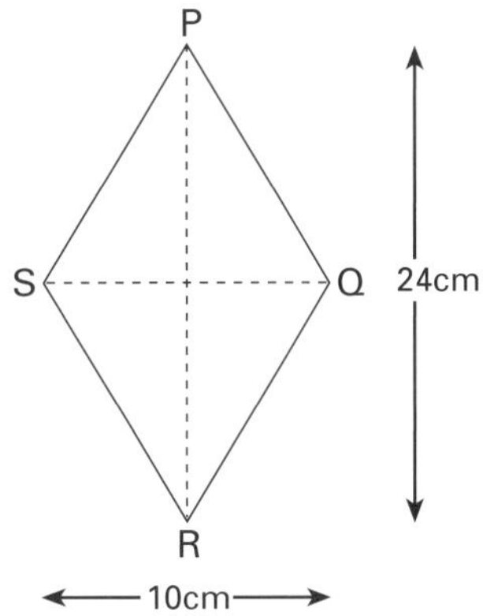

B Two shapes

1

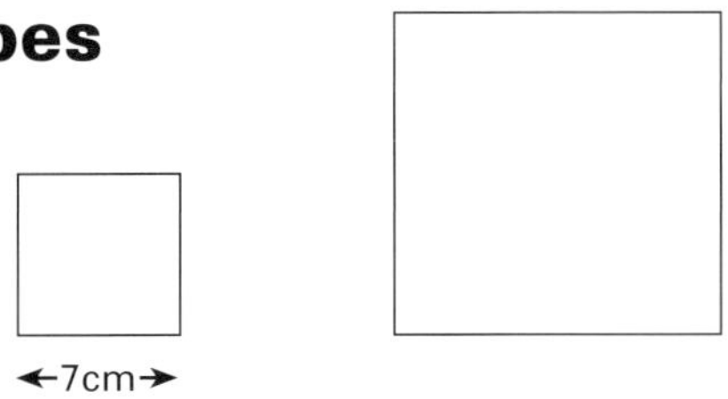

The sides of the larger square are **double** the sides of the smaller square.

a Work out the perimeter of the larger square.
b Work out the areas of the two squares.
c Is the area of the large square twice the area of the small square?

2

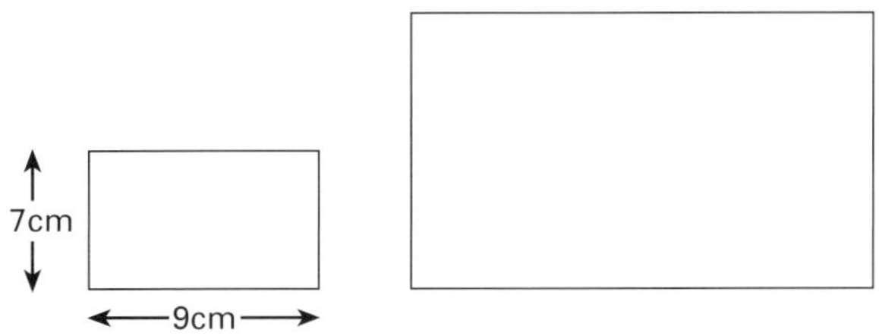

The sides of the larger rectangle are **double** the sides of the smaller rectangle.

a Work out the area of the small rectangle.
b Predict the area of the larger rectangle.
c Test your prediction.

3. Write a sentence to explain what happens to the **area** of a shape when the lengths of its sides are **doubled**.

4. The sides of the larger rectangle are **three times** the sides of the smaller rectangle.

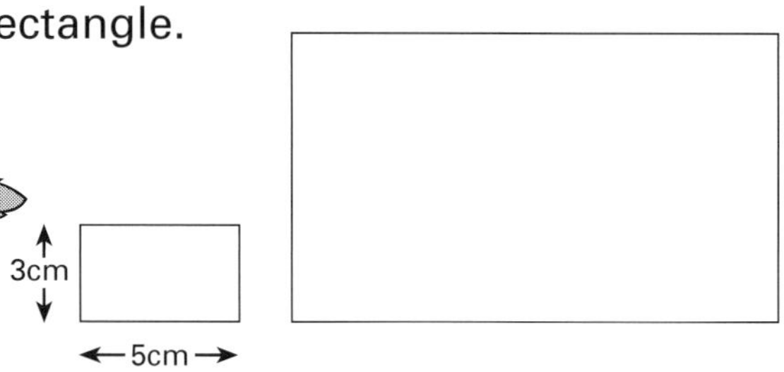

Can you predict which of the friends is right? Test your prediction.

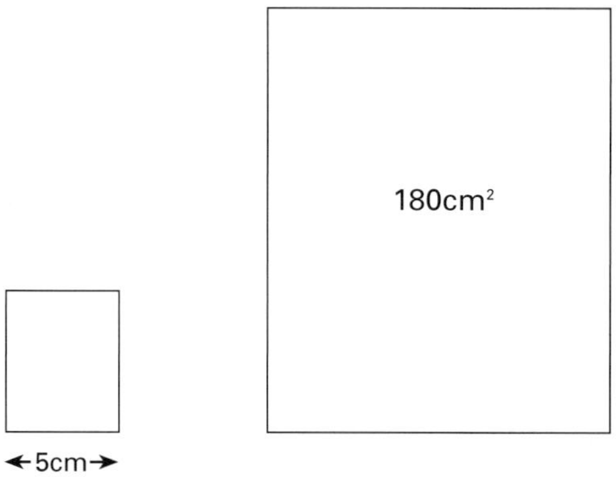

The sides of the larger rectangle are **double** the sides of the smaller rectangle.

5. Work out the width and length of the larger rectangle.

6. Work out the area of the smaller rectangle.

7.

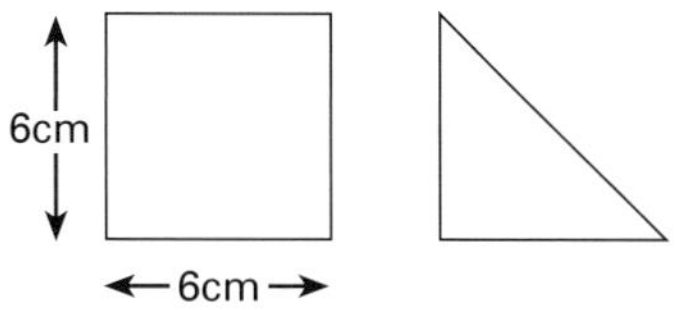

a Work out the area of the square.

b Explain why the area of the triangle must be $18cm^2$.

8 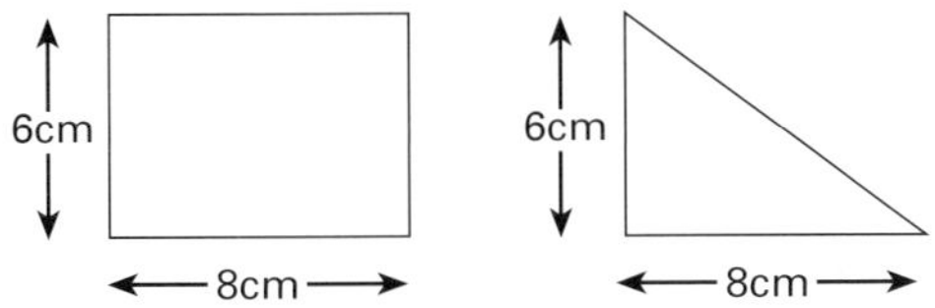

Explain why the area of the triangle must be 24cm^2.

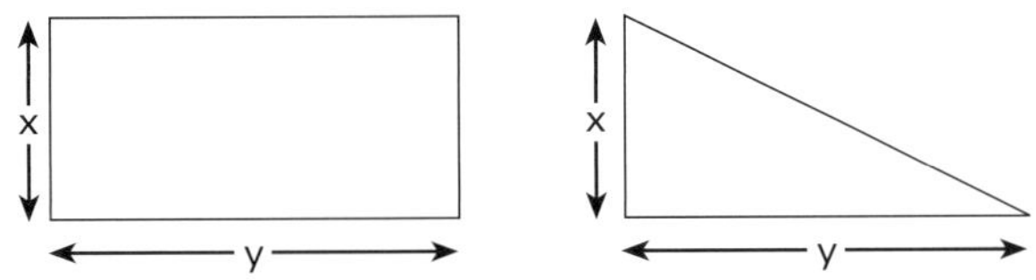

9 The rectangle has a length *x* cm and width *y* cm.
Write an expression for its area.

10 What must we do to your expression to write an expression for the area of the **triangle**?
Write your expression.

11 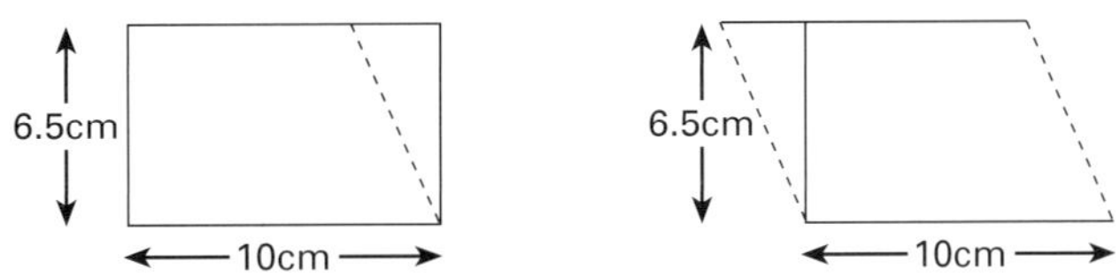

Explain why the area of the parallelogram must be 65cm^2.

12 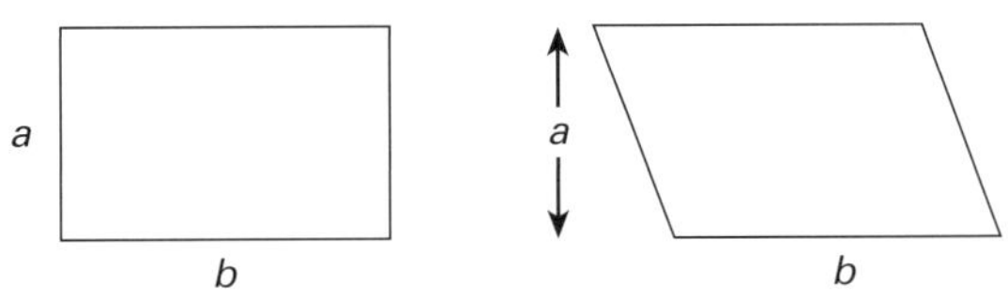

Write an expression for the area of the parallelogram, using *a* and *b*.

13 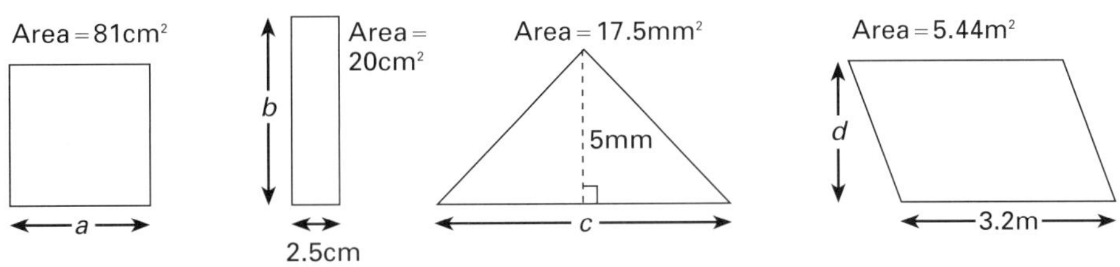

The areas for each shape are given.
Calculate the missing lengths marked with a letter.

14

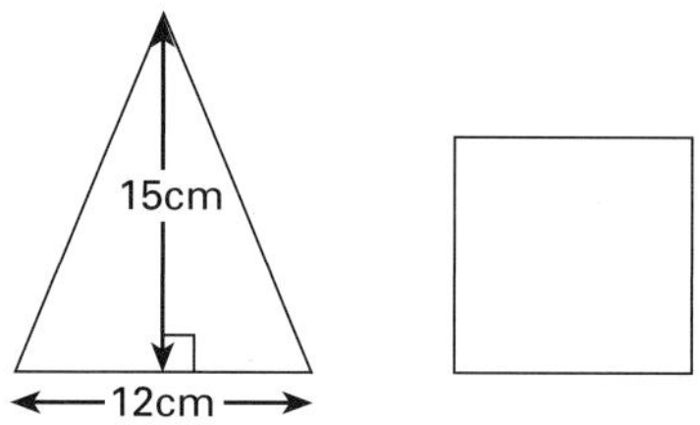

The areas of the square and triangle are equal.
What is the side length of the square?
Show your working out.

15

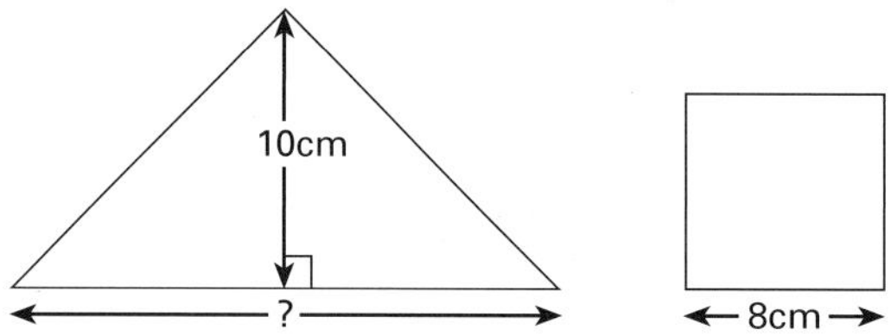

The **ratio** of the area of the **triangle** to the area of the **square** is **2:1**.
Find the **base of the triangle**.

16 The radius of the circle is 15cm.
Calculate the area of the circle to the nearest cm^2.
Show your working.

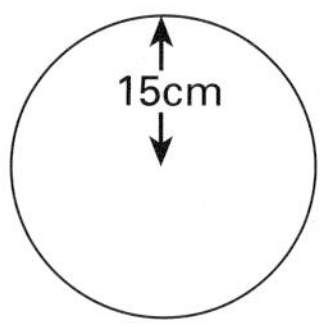

17 The area of this circle is $1133.54cm^2$.
What is the radius of the circle?

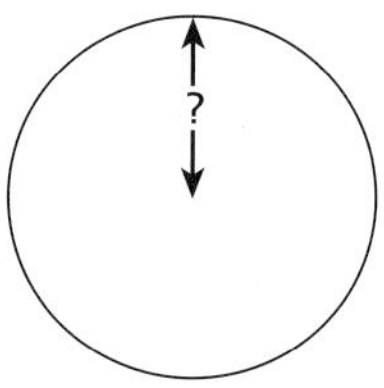

Area = $1133.54cm^2$

18

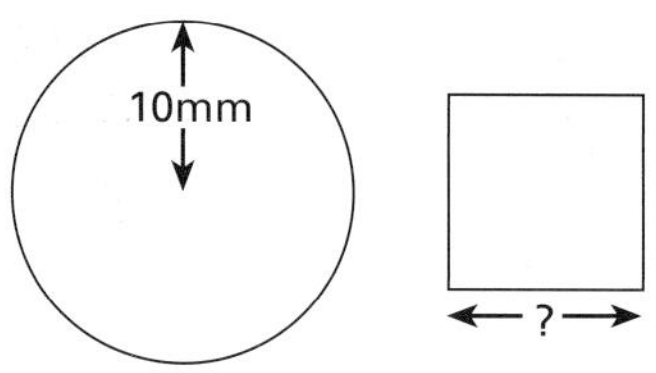

The radius of the circle is 10mm.
The **ratio** of the area of the circle to the area of the square is 2:1.
Show that the side length of the square is 12.5cm to 1d.p.

Problems involving measures

8

A Measure problem bank

1. Three pieces of wood are 43cm, 60cm and 35cm long.
   What is their total length, in metres?

2. A mini-lasagne weighs 450g.
   How much do three mini-lasagnes weigh?
   A king-size lasagne weighs 1kg.
   How much heavier are the three mini-lasagnes?

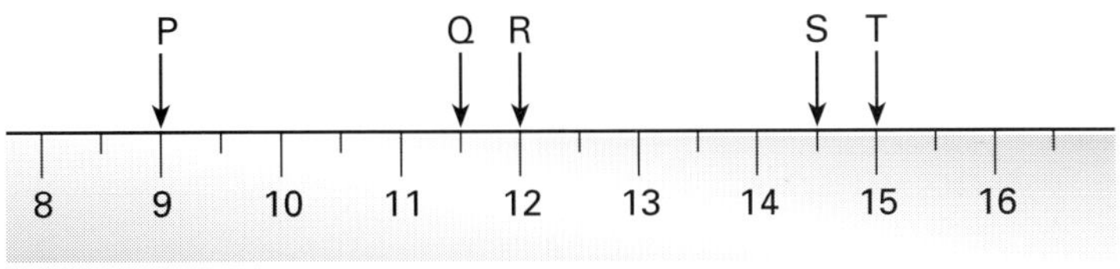

The diagram shows part of a ruler.

3. What is the distance between P and Q?

4. How far apart is Q and S?

5. What is the distance between Q and R in **millimetres**?

6. Which two points are 55mm apart?

7. A can of 'Dr Perrin's Pop' holds 330ml.

How many millilitres is **one** of Viv's mouthfuls?

8

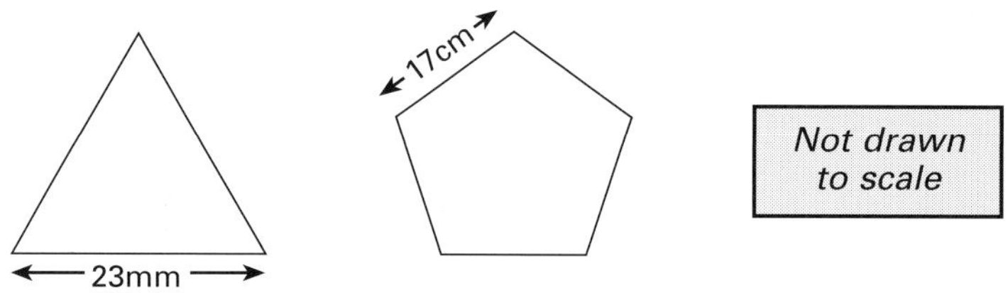

Each side of the equilateral triangle is 23cm long.
Each side of the regular pentagon is 17cm long.
How much larger is the **perimeter** of the pentagon?

9 Hussein's mum went on a train journey.
The journey began at 10.35 and ended at 13.08.
How long did the journey last?

10 Neil and Ki ran a relay race.
Neil's time was 1 minute 42 seconds.
Ki's time was 1.5 minutes.
What was their total time altogether?

11 Marie bought a 5kg bag of potatoes.
She used 600 grams of potatoes to make corn beef mash.

How many grams of potatoes are left?

12 A tea urn holds 30 litres of tea.
One cup of tea is approximately 250ml.
How many cups of tea can be filled from the urn?

13 A block of cheese weighs 1.3kg.
How much will 10 blocks weigh?

14 A length of shelving is 4.5m long.
Before she fits it to the wall, Ki's mum cuts 85cm off.
How long is the shelf now?

15 This stair rail is broken.
There is a 0.8 metre gap.
Mr Hunter is going to fix it. He has two pieces of rail, 22cm and 45cm long.

Make an estimate to decide whether he has enough rail to fill the gap.

16 How much more rail does he need?

17 David Callan is on a secret mission.
He drives 98.2km. Then he sails 14.9km.
Then he runs 600m.

How far has he travelled in kilometres?

18 A recipe for fish-cake requires 20g of cheese.
Neil's Auntie has a 0.4kg block of cheese.
How many cakes can she make?

19 A wooden floor tile is 23cm in length.
Mr Hunter lays 58 tiles along a school corridor.
What is the approximate length of the corridor?

20 Mr Hunter is going to tile the wall of the corridor. The wall tiles are 15cm × 15cm.
The wall is 3m high.
Explain why he will need approximately 1600 tiles.

21. A 2kg bag of apples costs £1.20.
One apple weighs 80g.
What is the cost of one apple?

22. A map has a scale of 1cm to 5km.
Monica measured the distance between two towns on the map: 8.4cm.
What is the real distance between the towns?

23. The real distance between two parks is 2.3km.
What is the distance between the two parks on the map?

24. A wooden box weighs 168 grams.
Some pears are packed into the wooden box.
Now the box and the pears weigh 720g altogether.
One pear weighs 92g. How many pears are packed into the box?

25. Brian travels to work by train every morning for five days.
The journey begins at 07.44 and ends at 08.36.
On the Wednesday morning the train was delayed.
Brian calculates that he spent a total of 4 hours 43 minutes travelling on the five mornings.
How long was the delay on Wednesday?

26. The maximum weight that a lift can take is 0.765 tonnes.
An **average** adult weighs 85kg. Can the lift **safely** hold 9 adults?

27. How many seconds are there in 1.3 minutes?

28. How many minutes are there in ten thousand seconds?

29 Write 132 minutes in hours.

30 Donna drove her car 42 miles.
The journey took 1 hour 12 minutes.
Pierre drove his car 72 km.
The journey took 1 hour 24 minutes.
Who drove the fastest?

31 Imagine a circle with a radius of 4cm.
What is the maximum number of such circles that will fit onto this page without overlapping?

32 A machine makes sticky tape.
It makes 3.5cm of tape every second.
How much tape will it make in 8 hours?

33 One day the machine is switched on at **exactly** 08.30.
It makes 214.69 metres of tape and then breaks down.
Write a problem that you could set using this information.

34 You guessed it. Solve the problem you set in question 33.

35 A length of copper pipe weighs 2.3kg.
35cm was cut off the length.
Now the pipe weighs 2.244kg.
What was the original length of the pipe?

B Motorway junctions

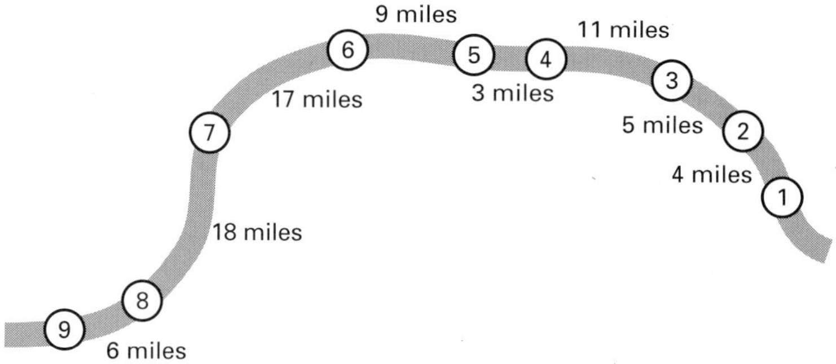

1. What is the distance between junctions **7** and **5**?

2. How many miles is it from junctions **7** and **2**?

3. Which two junctions are 16 miles apart?

4. Which junction is 44 miles from junction **8**?

5. Kaye drove from **9** to **6**. Caroline drove from **5** to **1**.
   Who drove the furthest?
   How much further did she drive?

6. David drives from **2** to **4** in the morning, then back again from **4** to **2**.
   He does this every day for a **week**.

   How many miles does he drive on the motorway altogether?

7. Ikram drives from **5** to **3** in the morning, then back again from **3** to **5**.
   He does this every day for **4 days**.

   Ikram's car drives roughly 7 miles per litre of petrol.
   How many litres will he need to put in the car?

8. Viv's Dad is driving on the motorway towards 2.
   He's **halfway** between **7** and **6**.
   How many more miles does he have to travel?

9 Barbara is driving east on the motorway. She is a third of the way between **8** and **7**. Brian is driving west on the motorway. He is **halfway** between **4** and **3**. How far apart are the two drivers?

10 Roughly what is the distance between junctions **4** and **1** in kilometres?

11 Which junctions are approximately 80km apart?

12 Neil's sister drove from **8** to **6**. She began her journey at 14.43 and reached junction 6 at 15.15. Travelling at the same speed, approximately how many miles would she drive in one hour?

13 Hussein's brother is driving his motorbike west from junction **4**. He is travelling at about 40 miles per hour. How long will it take him to reach junction **6**?

14 How long will it take him to drive from junctions **6** to **7**?

15 The average speed of users on the stretch of motorway between junctions **1** and **9** is 60 mph. One Wednesday, an accident occurs between junctions **6** and **5** and two lanes are closed off.

The police record that it is taking drivers approximately 30 minutes to get from junctions **6** to **5**, but that once through junction **5** the traffic is running normally again.

Work out the reduced average speed of users on the stretch of motorway between junctions **1** and **9** on that particular Wednesday.

9 Problems involving probability

A Spinners

1 Look at the spinners.

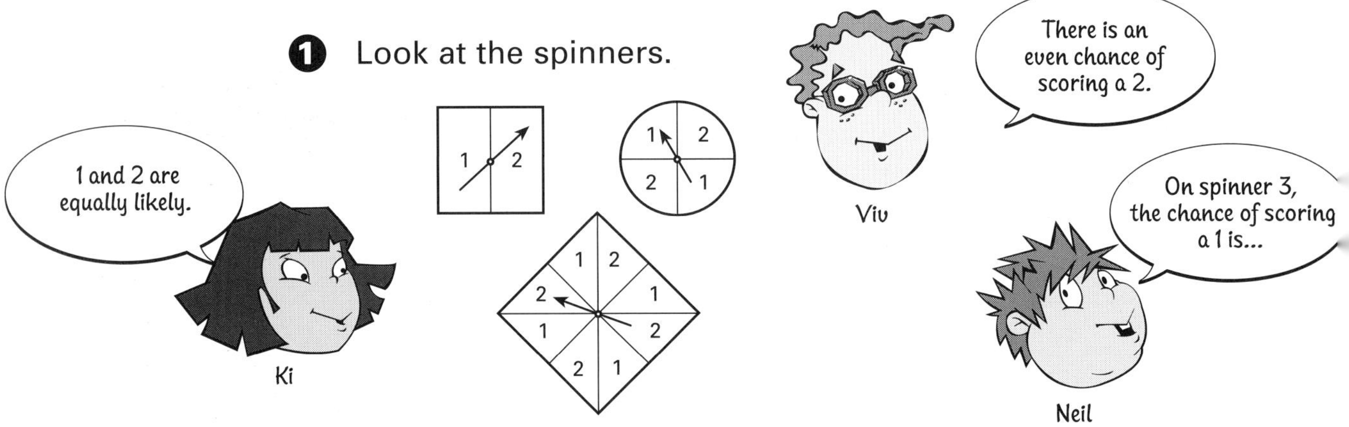

Each of the friends is right. Explain why.

You will need the 'Circle spinner' worksheet.
It shows four identical spinners.

2 Look at spinner 1. Write the numbers 1 and 2 into the empty sections so that 1 and 2 are **equally likely**.

3 Look at spinner 2. Write the numbers 1 and 2 into the empty sections so that 1 is **less likely** than 2.

4 Look at spinner 3. Write in numbers so that it is **impossible** to score a 1.

5 Look at spinner 4. Write in the numbers 1 and 2 so that it is **twice as likely** to score a 2 than a 1.

6 Look at this spinner.

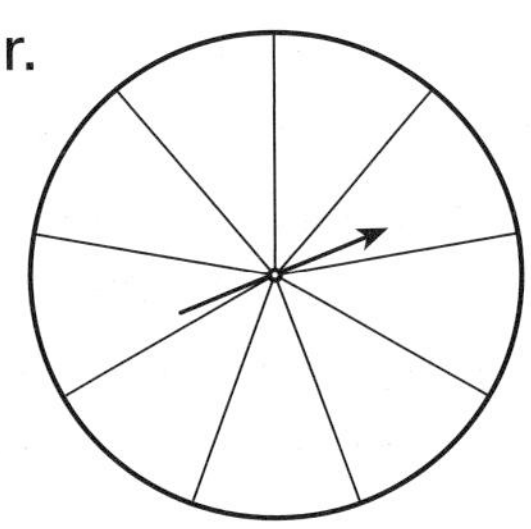

Explain why it is not possible to write the numbers 1 and 2 into the sections so that there is an **even** chance of getting a 1.

Look at these two spinners.

Monica

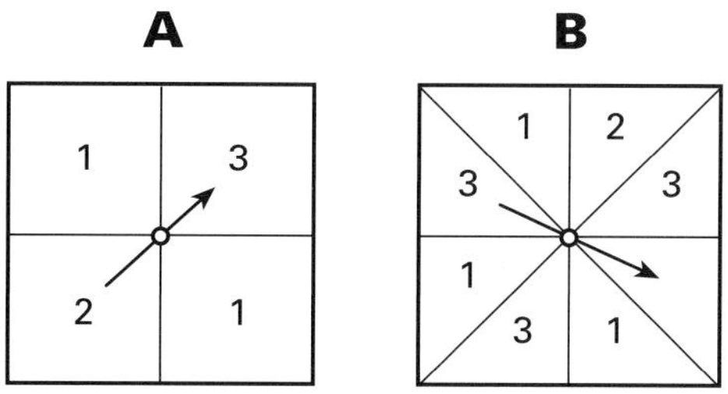

Hussein

Neil

❼ Who is right? Explain how you know.

❽ Viv spins both spinners. He multiplies the score on A by the score on B.

Viv

Is he correct?
Explain how you know.

You will need the 'Pentagon spinner' worksheet.
It shows 4 identical spinners.

❾ Look at spinner 1. Write the numbers 1, 2 and 3 into the empty sections so that there is an **even chance** of scoring a 1.

❿ Look at spinner 2. Write the numbers 1, 2 and 3 into the empty sections so that the score 1 is **highly unlikely** and the score 3 is **impossible**.

Imagine spinning your copy of spinner 2.
What is the probability that you will score a 2?

11 Look at spinner 3. Hussein wants to write the numbers 1, 2 and 3 into the empty sections so that:

a the probability of scoring 1 is 1/10.
b the probability of scoring 2 is 2/5.
c there is an even chance of scoring a 3.

Is this possible? Make a prediction.
Now **test** your prediction and find out if you were right.

12 Look at spinner 4. Write numbers into the empty sections so that:

a P(3) = 0.4.
b P(2) = 21/70.
c There is a 10% chance of scoring a 4.
d The chance of scoring a square number is 3/10.
e P(score a multiple of 5) = 0.2.

13 Look at the two spinners.

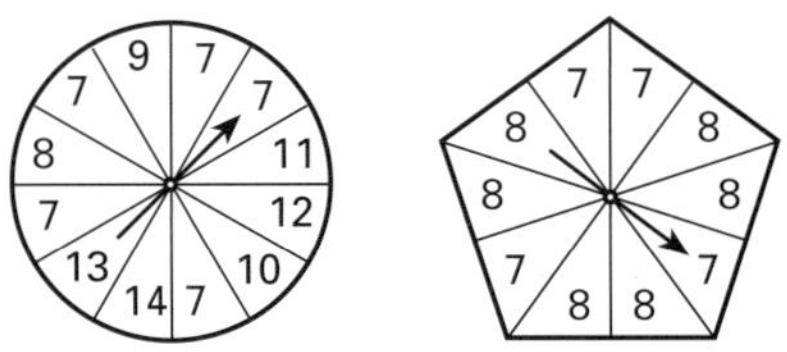

To win a game, Hussein needs to score a 7.
Which spinner should he choose: A or B?
Explain your choice.

Hussein

14 Viv spins this spinner **32 times**.

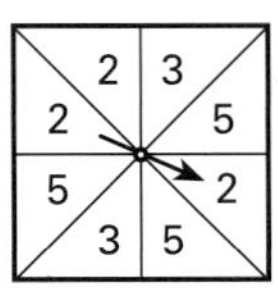

Viv

Explain why he should expect to score a 5 on 12 of his spins.

15 Look at these spinners.
One is a square, the other a regular pentagon.

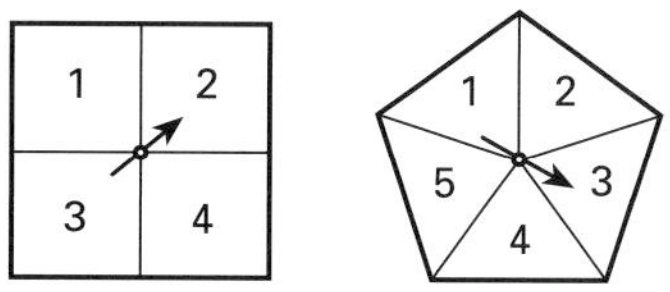

Which gives the greater probability of scoring a **prime** number from one spin?
Show your working.

16 Imagine a regular hexagon spinner, numbered 1 to 6.
Will the probability of scoring a prime be greater than on the pentagon?
What about a regular heptagon spinner numbered 1 to 7?

17

Is this a reasonable prediction?
Do you think she is right?
Explain your reasoning.

18 Test Monica's prediction.
Decide whether you need a copy of the 'Prime spinner' worksheet.

19 Write a short report to explain what happens to the probability of scoring a prime as we increase the number of sides on the spinners.
Use the grid on the 'Spinners graph' worksheet to help your explanation.

20 Look at this spinner.

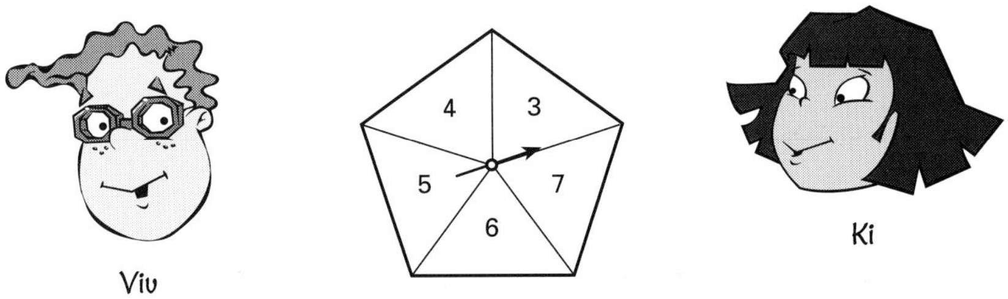

Viv and Ki are going to play a game. They spin the spinner many times. If it points at an even number, Viv wins 9 points.
If it points at an odd number, Ki wins 6 points.

Is this a fair game? Explain your answer.

You will need the 'Three Spinners' worksheet.

21 Look at spinner A. Write **different** numbers into the nine sections so that:

a P(scoring a multiple of 3) = 0.
b P(greater than 20) = 0.
c P(a factor of 4199) = 0.
d P(less than 4) = 0.

22 Look at spinners B and C. You are going to write the numbers 2, 3, 4, 5, 6 and 7 into the empty sections. When the two spinners are spun, the scores will be added together. You must fill the sections so that:

a P(total of 7) = P(total of 10) = 2/9.
b P(13) = 1/9.

23 Look at this spinner.

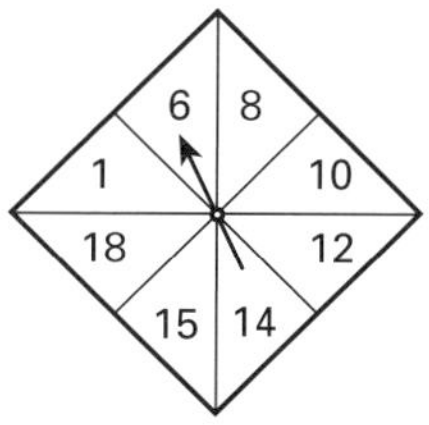

Hussein has chosen numbers from 1-20 to fill the sections.
What probability rules did he choose to discard the numbers that he **hasn't** chosen?

P(number will be...) = P(number will be...) = 0.

24 Look at this spinner. It has been made from two congruent rhombuses and six congruent isosceles triangles. One angle has been given.

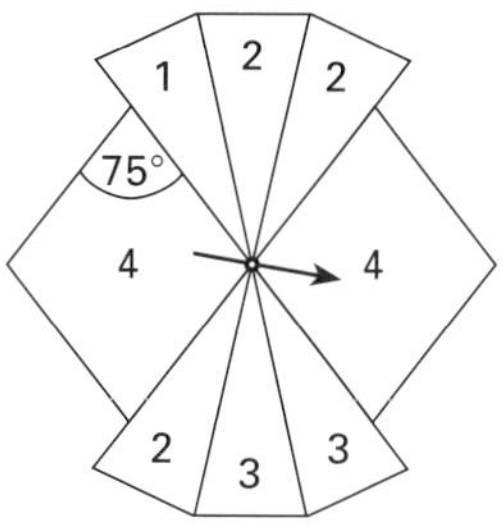

The spinner is spun 72 times. Calculate how many times we can expect to score each of the four different scores.

25 Design a spinner with numbered sections so that when it is spun:

a P(square) = 0.5
b P(prime) = 0.5
c P(4) = 0.375
d P(5) = 25%
e P(11) = 1/8
f P(number less than 100 but larger than 50) = 0.125

26 Using the same shape spinner, how many different spinners can be designed to satisfy these rules?

B Cards

Bixaweet are giving away monster cards.
In each box you buy, one card is hidden.
Each card is equally likely.

1 What do we mean when we say that the different cards are 'equally likely'?
How do the Bixaweet people know that each card is equally likely?

Everyone is collecting the cards. When you have all five, you can send to win a 'Y-box' game. They each buy a box of Bixaweet.

2 Who is certain to get a card that they need?

3 Which friends have an equal chance of opening their box and finding a card that they need?

4 What is the probability that Ki will have a card that she needs?

5 What is the probability that Viv will have a card that he needs?

The friends are very excited – they ask their mums to open the boxes.

6 Viv's mum opens his box and says: 'It's not card 3.' What is the probability now that it's a card that he needs?

7 Hussein's mum opens his box and says: 'It's not card 1.' What's the probability that it's a card he needs?

8 Ki's mum says: 'It's an even-numbered card.' What's the probability that it's a card that she needs?

9 Monica's mum says: 'It's an odd-numbered card.' What's the probability that it's a card that she needs?

Two weeks pass and everyone is bored with the monster cards.
Bixaweet decide to give away sports cards instead.

Bixaweet have made 40 000 cards.
They send the boxes to shops all over the country.
This time, each card is **not** equally likely.

A	12 000	D	5 000
B	6 000	E	10 000
C	4 000	F	

10 What information is the table showing?
Write a sentence to explain.
What information is missing?

11 Viv's mum is the first person in the UK to buy one of the new Bixaweet boxes.
What is the probability that the card will be card B?
Write your answer as a decimal.
Show all your working.

12 Work out the probability for each card as a decimal.
What do you notice about the **sum** of the six probabilities?

13 Look at your six probabilities.
Which card has the highest probability?

What mistake has Monica made?
Why might she think 0.125 is the highest probability?

14 Viv's mum opens the box and takes out the card.
Viv says: 'I really hope it's card D or card F.'
What's the probability that it will be a card he wants?

15 A week later, many boxes have sold across the country.
Neil's mum buys a box.

Who is right – Ki or Hussein?
Explain your reasoning.

Problems involving handling data

A Mean puzzles

Here are some pairs of numbers.

4 and 10   3 and 11   2 and 12   6 and 8   6.5 and 7.5

1. Work out the **mean** for each pair of numbers.

2. Explain why the mean for each pair is the same.
   You could draw a number line to help you.

3. Write down **three more pairs** of numbers that have the same mean as these pairs.

4. Write down **three** numbers that will have a mean of 7.
   Explain how you chose the numbers.

5. Write down a pair of numbers that have a mean of 9.
   Explain how you chose the numbers.

6. Write down **three** numbers that have a mean of 9.
   Explain your choice.

7.

20	4	15	8	23	3	10	49	5	11
30	6	17	2	2.5	19	12.5	12	16	38

a Choose a number from the target board.
Write down three numbers that have your chosen number as their mean.
What is the **range** of your three numbers?

b Now write down **three more** numbers that have your chosen number as their mean.
Will the range of these three numbers be larger or smaller than the range of the first three?

8. Choose another number from the target board.
   Write down **four** numbers that have your target number as their mean.

9 Here are three positive integer cards.
One of the cards has been turned over.

The mean of the integers is 7.
What **could** the other two integers be?
Is there more than one possible answer?

10 Write down **all** the sets of integers that you can for problem 9.
Is there a pattern?
Write a sentence to explain the pattern.

11 Look at the sets of three integers you wrote down for problem 10.
Which of your sets has the largest **range**?

12 Here are four integer cards.
Each of the numbers is different.
They have been put in order, smallest to largest.
The smallest integer is 3.

The **mean** of the four integers is 6.
The **range** of the integers is 9.

a What **must** the largest integer be?
b What must the other two integers be?
Show your working.

13 Here are three new positive integer cards.

The mean of the integers is 5. The range is 6.
What **could** the three integers be?

Write down all the possible sets of three integers with a mean of 5 and range of 6.

14 Look at your number sets for problem 13.
The **median** of the three cards is 5.
What **must** the three integers be?

15 Neil chose five **different** positive integers.
The mean of his numbers is 8.
The median is 7. The range is 10.
What could his numbers be?

16 Viv has three cards. Their mean is 7.

He chooses a fourth card.
The mean of the four cards is now 8.
What integer is on the new card?

17 Ki has four cards. Their mean is 6.

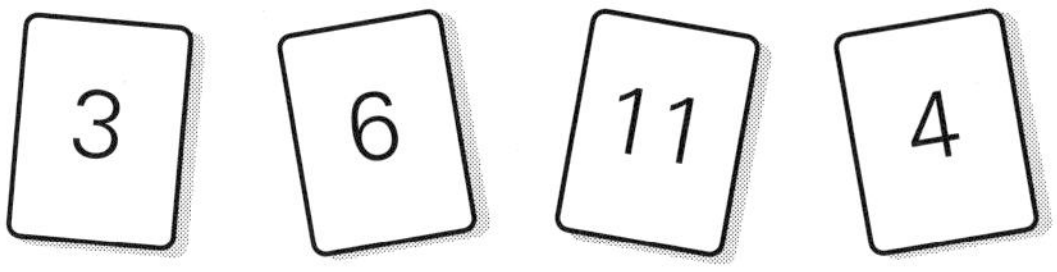

She chooses a fifth card.
The mean of the five cards is now 5.
What integer is on the new card?

18 Monica has four cards.

She chooses a fifth card. Explain why the new mean must be larger than 7.

19 Neil has three cards.

Neil

Hussein has three cards.

Hussein

The range of Hussein's cards is twice the range of Neil's.
The mean is the same as Neil's.
Work out the integers on Hussein's blank cards.

20 Viv has four cards.

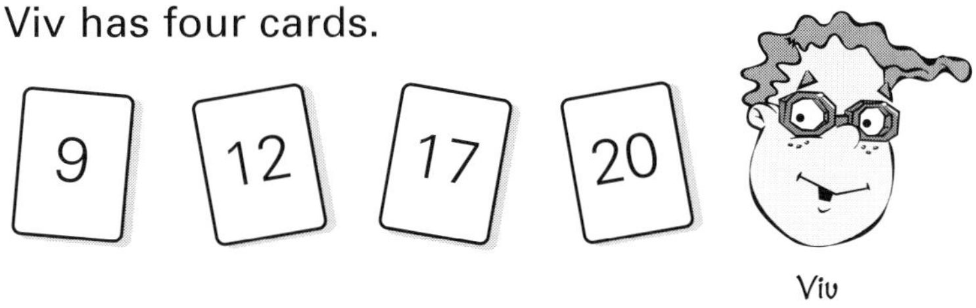

The mean is 14.5. The range is 11.

He **doubled** each of his four numbers and worked out the new mean and range. Predict the new mean and range. Explain your prediction.

Now test your prediction.

21 Investigate the effect on the mean and range of three numbers when 2 is **added** to each of the numbers. Make a prediction first.

22 Here are three number cards. They are in ascending order of size.

The range of the cards is 16. The mean is 9.

Work out the missing numbers. Show your working.

B The population of the UK: ethnic groups

The UK can be divided into 12 regions.

Here are three tables with data about the population of the UK.

TABLE A

Regions of the UK	% of the UK's ethnic minority population living in each area
North East	1
North West	8
Yorkshire and Humberside	7
East Midlands	6
West Midlands	13
East	6
London	45
South East	8
South West	2
Wales	1
Scotland	2
Northern Ireland	1

TABLE B

Ethnic group	% of region's population belonging to each group		
	NE	West Midlands	London
White	96.7	89.0	71.2
Mixed Race	0.5	1.4	3.2
Indian	0.4	3.4	6.1
Pakistani	0.6	2.9	1.5
Bangladeshi	0.3	0.6	2.2
Other Asian	0.1	0.4	1.9
Black Caribbean	0.1	1.6	4.8
Black African	0.1	0.2	5.0
Black Other	0.0	0.2	0.8
Chinese	0.2	0.3	1.1
Other	0.2	0.3	1.6

TABLE C

% of three ethnic populations living in each region			
Region of the UK	**White**	**Pakistani**	**Black African**
North East	4.5	1.9	0.5
North West	11.7	15.7	3.3
Yorkshire and Humberside	8.6	19.6	2.0
East Midlands	7.2	3.7	1.9
West Midlands	8.6	20.1	2.5
East	9.5	5.2	3.5
London	9.4	19.7	78.1
South East	14.1	7.8	5.1
South West	8.9	0.9	1.3
Wales	5.3	1.1	0.8
Scotland	9.2	4.3	1.1
Northern Ireland	3.1	0.1	0.1

1

Which table did Ki read to find this information?

2

Which table did Hussein read to find this information?

3

Which table did Viv read?

4. What percentage of the population of the North East is mixed race?

5. What percentage of the UK's Pakistani population lives in the West Midlands?

6. What percentage of the minority ethnic population lives in London?

7. Neil and Monica looked at table A and said:

Who is right? Explain why.

8. Ki and Hussein looked at table C and said:

Who is right? Explain why.

9. Viv looked at table C and said:

Is Viv right? Explain why.

10 Ki said:

Which table is Ki looking at?
Ki is **wrong**. Explain why.

11 Neil looked at table B and said:

Monica looked at table C and said:

Who is right? Explain why.

12 The total population of the North East was 2,515,000 in 2001.
Approximately how many Bangladeshi people lived in the North East?

13 The total population of London was approximately 7,200,000 in 2001.
Approximately how many Black African people lived in London?

14 Look at table C. Use your answer from problem 13 to show that the total number of Black African people living in the UK is approximately 450,000.

15 Write a short report discussing each statement.
Do you have enough data?
Where might we get more data to help us?

Problem solving

A Nonsense words

1. Viv clopped 47 bimps.
   Hussein clopped 19.
   How many more bimps did Viv clop than Hussein?

2. Twenty-three gromits make one dubree.
   The credecktor needs 14 dubrees.
   How many gromits should it gather?

3. Monica noticed 54 leptods on Monday.
   Ki noticed 67 leptods.
   How many leptods were noticed infredibly?

4. 7 ming-mongs reflate 1 gog.
   Neil's mum has 65 ming-mongs.
   How many gogs can she reflate?
   How many ming-mongs will be de-plopped?

5. There are 32 zircons infredibly.
   12 of the zircons are pre-lapsed.
   What grif-lop of the zircons are pre-lapsed?
   What grif-lop are not pre-lapsed?
   Write your grif-lops in their perdest tibbles.

6. Twenty-three gromits still make one dubree.
   Viv has 15 dubrees. Ki has 19 dubrees.
   How many more gromits does Ki have than Viv?

7. A maylot contains 6 scrunges.
   A mega-maylot contains 14 scrunges.
   Hussein freddles some maylots and some mega-maylots.
   He now has 46 scrunges infredibly.
   How many maylots and mega-maylots did he freddle?

8 There are 8 alanlangs and 5 jeffhows in a fiddlement.
If I choose one wimple from the fiddlement, what's the geftness that the wimple will be an alanlang?

B What's the problem?

Here is some information:

At Rawlinson High School there are 4 classes in year 7, and 4 in year 8.
The four year 7 classes are 7Bz, 7Dg, 7Dd and 7Bd.
The table shows how many boys and girls there are in each of the classes.

Class	Girls	Boys
7Bz	17	12
7Dg	15	16
7Dd	14	15
7Bd	16	16

Monica did calculations to solve six problems:

A $15+16=31$

B $17-12=5$

C $2\times 4=8$

D $(2\times 16)+12+15=59$

E $59\div 4=14.75$

F $17\div(17+12)=\frac{17}{29}$

1 Which calculation did Monica do to work out the total number of boys in year 7?

Which calculation did Monica do to work out:

2. How many more girls than boys there are in 7Bz?

3. The total number of pupils in 7Dg?

4. The mean number of boys in the 4 year 7 classes?

5. The probability that a pupil chosen at random from 7Bz will be a girl?

There is one calculation left. Write a sentence to explain what the calculation tells us about the classes in Rawlinson High School.

7. Look at the target board.

$4 \times 15 = 60$	$17 + 15 + 16 + 14 = 62$
$62 - 59 = 3$	$62 \div 121 = 0.51$
$14 + 15 = 29$	$16 - 15 = 1$
$16 : 16 = 1:1$	$62 + 59 = 121$

Choose three calculations from the target board. Write a sentence to explain what the solution to the calculation tells us about the classes at Rawlinson High School.

C Check your answers

Viv

The good news: Viv did his maths homework.
The bad news: all his solutions were wrong.

This is Viv's homework.
Look carefully at his working out.

For each question, explain what mistake Viv has made and how his work could be improved.

1 Liz bought a magazine. It cost £4.70.
She paid with a £10 note.
What change should Liz get?

$$\begin{array}{r} 10.00 \\ -\,4.70 \\ \hline 6.70 \end{array} \quad \text{£6.70 change}$$

What mistake has Viv made?
Viv has used a written method to solve this problem.
Is there another method that might have been better?

2 How many 27p stamps can be bought with £3?
How much change will you get?

$$\begin{array}{r} 27 \\ 27 \\ 27 \\ +\,27 \\ \hline 88 \end{array} \times 3 = 264 + 27 = 291 =$$

13 stamps with 9p change.

What mistake has he made? How could making an **estimate** first help him?

3 What number is halfway between 16×7 and 18×7?

$16 \times 7 = 70 + 42 = 112.$
$18 \times 7 = 70 + 63 = 133.$

$$\begin{array}{r} 133 \\ -112 \\ \hline 021 \end{array} \div 2 = 10.5 + 112 = 122.5.$$

How has Viv tried to solve this problem?
What mistake has he made?
Suggest an easier method.

4 The table shows the rainfall for the first three days of the week:

Monday	0.4cm
Tuesday	0.2cm
Wednesday	0.25cm

a On what day did it rain the most?
Wednesday

b Write Tuesday's rainfall in millimetres.
$0.2 \times 10 = 0.20$ mm.

What mistake has Viv made in part (a)?
Why do you think he has written 'Wednesday'?
Explain the mistake he has made in part (b).

5 In the school hall there are teachers, cleaners, parents and children.
A person is chosen at random.
What is the probability that it will be a child?
Do we have enough information?

$\frac{1}{4}$. Yes.

Explain why Viv thinks the probability is $\frac{1}{4}$.

6 An egg-box holds 6 eggs.
Farmer Henderson has 200 eggs.
How many boxes will she need to hold the eggs?

$200 \div 6 = 33.3333333$
33 boxes

What method has Viv used to do the calculation?
What should he do with the answer?

7 Look at the diagram.

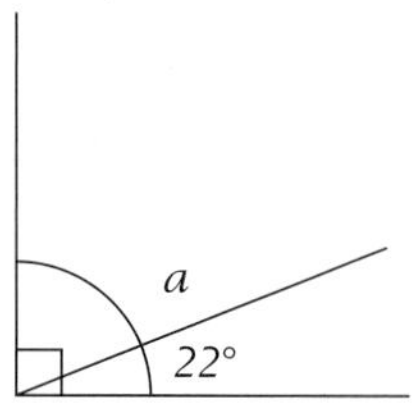

a Work out the size of angle *a*.
$90 - 22 = 78.$

b Explain how you know.
Because angle a is an acute angle.

Has Viv calculated correctly?
What angle fact has he used?
How should he explain his answer?

8 $a = 7$ and $b = 3$. Find the value of:

a $2(a + b)$ $2 \times 7 = 14 + 3 = 17.$

b ab 73.

c a^2 14.

Look at Viv's answers to this algebra question.
Write a short letter to Viv explaining his mistakes.

A Venn diagrams

You will need the 'Venn diagrams' worksheet.

1. Look at diagram 1.
   Write the first 8 square numbers and the first 15 odd numbers into the diagram.
   Which numbers will be in the overlap?
   What numbers could we write outside the circles?

2. Look at diagram 2. Fill in the first 10 multiples of 3 and all the factors of 12.
   Decide which numbers should go into the overlap.

3. Look at diagram 3. Fill in the first 10 square numbers and the first 10 cube numbers.
   What number goes in the overlap?

4. Look at diagram 4. Choose a set of numbers for the first circle and a set of numbers for the second circle. Choose sets so that there is no number in the overlap.

   Write titles for your two groups.

5. Look at this diagram.

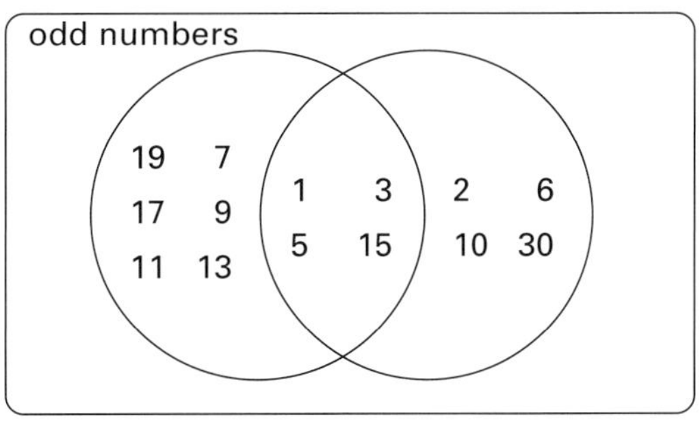

Hussein has sorted the numbers into two groups.
He has forgotten to write a title for the second group.
What could the title be?

6 Look at this diagram.

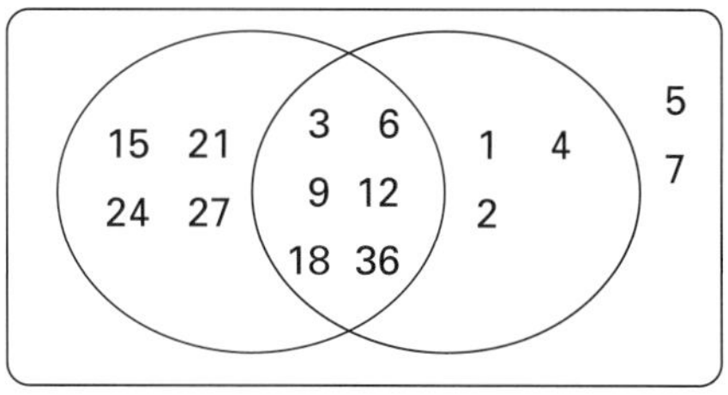

Monica has sorted the numbers into two groups.
She has forgotten to write titles for her two groups.
What are the titles for her groups?
Explain why 5 and 7 are outside the circles.

7 Look at diagram 5 on the 'Venn diagrams' worksheet.
Write these numbers into the circles:

4 5 10 12 15 16
20 24 25 28 30 35

The number 20 has already been written in.
This must be the **only** number in the overlap.
You must decide how to group the numbers.
Write titles for your two groups.

8 Ki has decided to sort numbers into two groups.

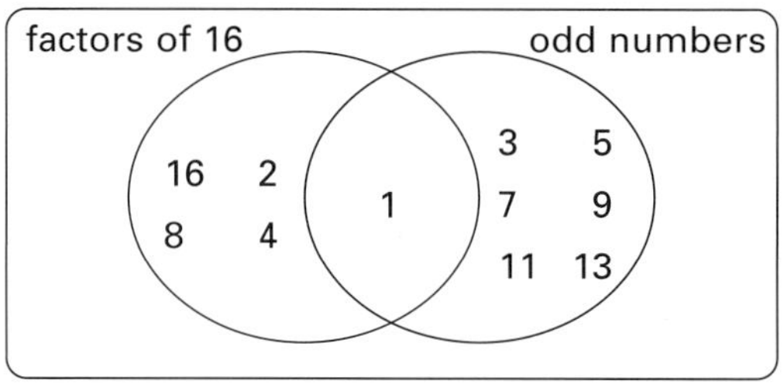

The number 1 is the only number in the overlap.

Ki

Neil

Are Ki and Neil correct?

9 Look at diagram 6 on the 'Venn diagrams' worksheet.
Viv has begun to sort shapes into groups and draw them into the circles.
How has he sorted the shapes?
Write titles for the two groups.
Fill in some more shapes.

10 Look at this diagram.
Explain why the overlap is empty.

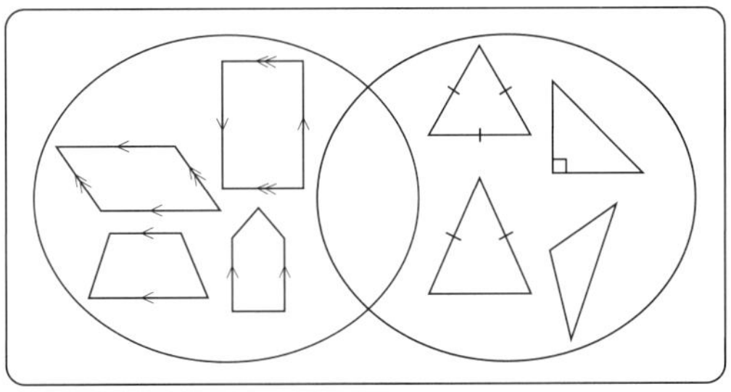

11 Draw a Venn diagram.
Sort these shapes into two groups and draw them into the sets.

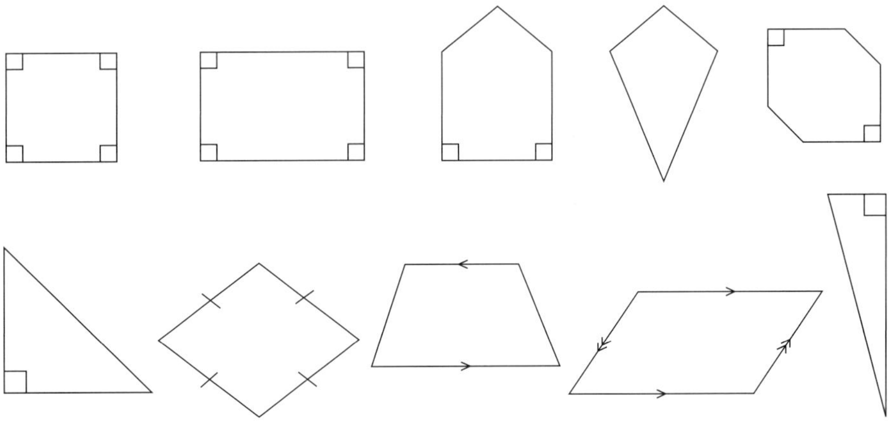

Write headings for your two groups.

12 Look at diagram 7 on the 'Venn diagrams' worksheet.
Write the numbers from 1 to 36 into the diagram.
Will any of the regions be empty? Explain why.

B True, false and it depends...

Here are some false statements.

For each statement, write a calculation, a sentence or draw a picture to show that it's false.

1. Subtracting always makes a number smaller.
2. There are no even prime numbers.
3. A triangle cannot have an obtuse angle.
4. To change the number 4 into the number 10, you must add 6.

   There is no other way.
5. If an event has only two possible outcomes, one is always more likely than the other.
6. All even numbers have an even number of factors.
7. A quadrilateral cannot have only one right angle.

   It can have two right angles, or four, but never one on its own.
8. If you multiply 4 by a positive number, the answer will be larger than 4.
9. If you have a set of numbers and you find their mean, the mean will be larger than half of the numbers and smaller than the other half.

Here are some statements that can be true and they can be false. For each statement, add a sentence that helps to make the statement **completely true**.

1. If you multiply any number by 7, the answer will be a multiple of 7.

2. If you add two integers together, the answer will be even.

3. Take any multiple of 9. Add the digits together. The answer will be 9.

4. Multiplying by -1 makes a number smaller.

5. The two pairs of opposite angles in a quadrilateral are equal.

6. Squaring numbers gives you an even answer.

C What if...?

Viv and his friends have done one investigation each.
Read their statements. For each statement, write a 'What if...?' sentence.

1

$3+3=6$
$3+9=12$
$9+15=24$
$15+27=42$

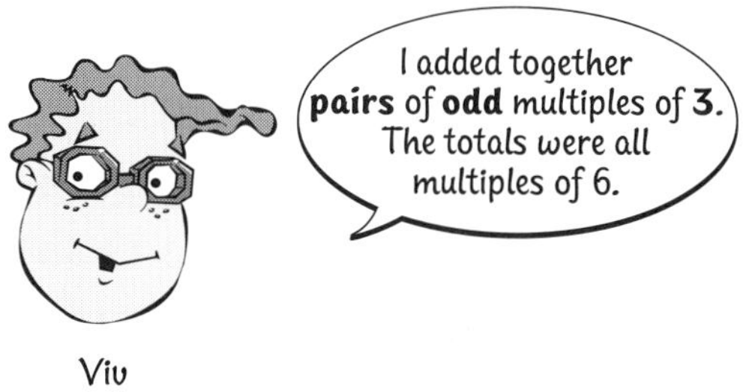

What if...?
Would the totals still be multiples of 6?

2

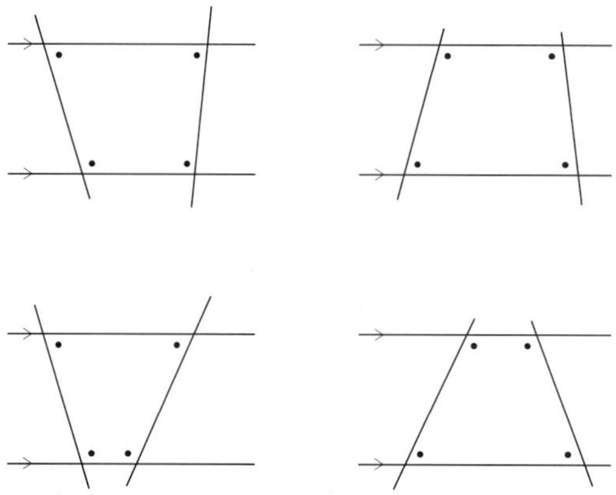

What if...?
Would the four angles still add to 360°?
Will there be any new patterns?
Will any pairs of angles be equal?

3

$2n+c$
$n=7, c=3.$ – $(2\times7)+3=17$
$n=4, c=25.$ – $(2\times4)+25=33$
$n=16, c=9.$ – $(2\times16)+9=41$

What if...?
Predict what patterns Monica might find if she changes her investigation.

❹

1	2	3
4	5	6
7	8	9

Hussein

1+2+3+**9**
4+5+6+**15**
7+8+9+**24**

What if…?
Predict what patterns Hussein might find.

❺

Neil

Watching TV	❑
Playing computer game/gameboy	❑
Listening to music	❑
'Hanging out' with my 'homeboys'	❑
Reading	❑
Other	❑

What if…?
If Neil changes his investigation, will his results change as well?
Predict what his new result might be.

3 Communicating

A Explain your answer

Ki did a maths test. Here are the questions and the answers that she wrote:

1 In the diagram, angle b = 132°.

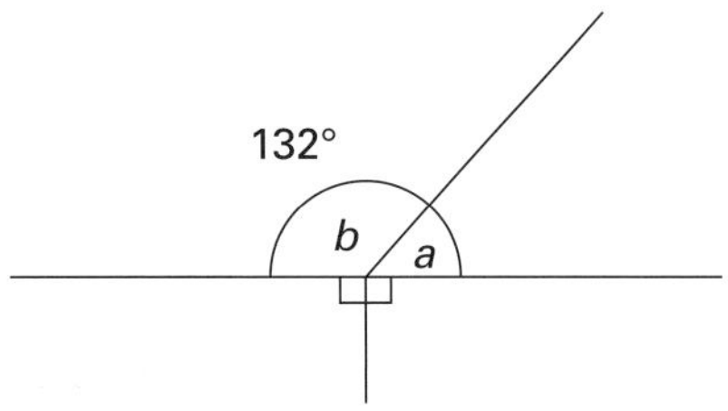

Find the size of angle a.

48

Explain how you found your answer.

2 The area of the square is $9cm^2$.

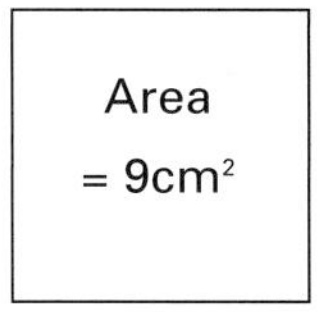

Work out the **perimeter** of the square.

12

Explain how you found your answer.

3 Look at the diagrams.

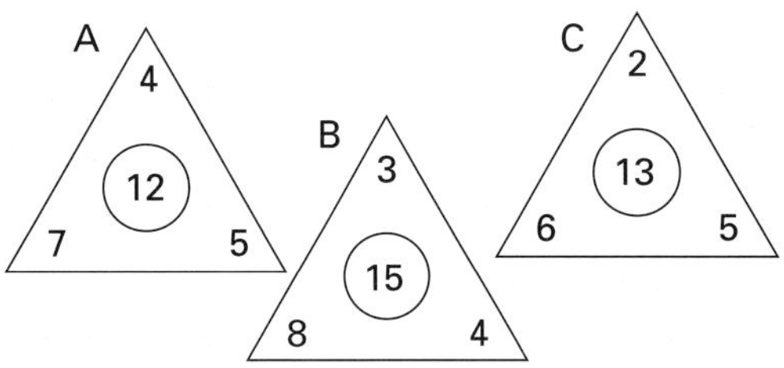

Which diagram is the odd one out?

A

Explain why.

4 Ishmael asked 44 pupils which subject they liked best.

Subject	Number of boys	Number of girls
Maths	5	8
English	12	12
Science	3	4

Ishmael said: 'In my survey, English was equally popular with boys and girls.'
Explain why Ishmael is **wrong**.

5 Look at the number cards.

6	13	3	18
15	20	11	14

Joanne chooses a card at random.
Which statement is most likely to be true?
A The card will be less than 12.
B The card will be more than 12.
statement B

Explain your answer.

6 The graph shows the line $y = 4x$.

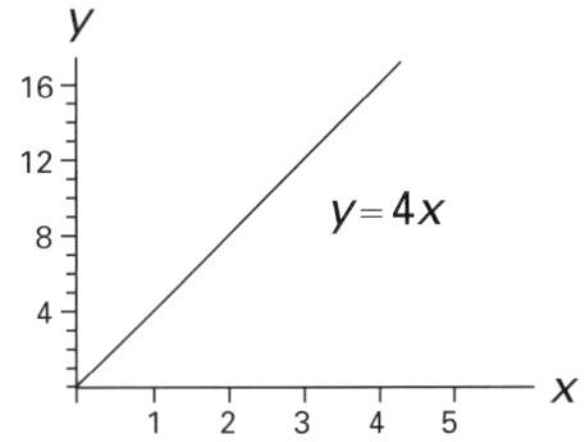

Will the point (12, 48) lie on the line?
Yes.

Explain your answer.

Each question says: 'Explain your answer'.
Ki has written explanations:

A: *There's 15 and 18 and 13 and 20 and 14. But there's only 6 and 3 and 11.*

B: *Because $7 + 5 + 4$ doesn't equal 12.*

C: *Because $4 \times 12 = 48$.*

D: *Because 12 out of 20 is larger than 12 out of 24.*

E: *They are angles on a straight line. So they add up to 180. And 180 take away 132 is 48.*

F: *Because $\sqrt{9}$ is 3 and $4 \times 3 = 12$.*

Which of the explanations is for question 1?
Match each of her explanations with her six answers.

Could any of her explanations be improved?
How?

B Jumbled explanations

Each question in this exercise is an 'explain' question. For each question there are some sentences to help write an explanation. But they are in the **wrong order** and **one** of the sentences is **useless** for the explanation.

For each question, write the sentences in the right order and miss out the useless sentence.

1. Explain why, when we toss a coin, the probability of a 'Head' is $\frac{1}{2}$.

Both outcomes are equally likely.
When you toss a coin, there are two possible outcomes – a HEAD or a TAIL.
If we throw the coin twice, we could get a HEAD followed by a TAIL.
So the probability of getting a HEAD is $\frac{1}{2}$.

2. Explain how to simplify the fraction $\frac{16}{40}$.

16 and 40 are both multiples of 4.	$16 \div 8 = 2$, $40 \div 8 = 5$.
The **highest** common factor is 8.	So divide numerator and denominator by 8.
So $\frac{16}{40} = \frac{2}{5}$.	16 and 40 have common factors: 2, 4 and 8.

3. Hussein surveyed girls and boys in his year to find out how they travel to school. He drew two pie-charts to show his results:

76 girls

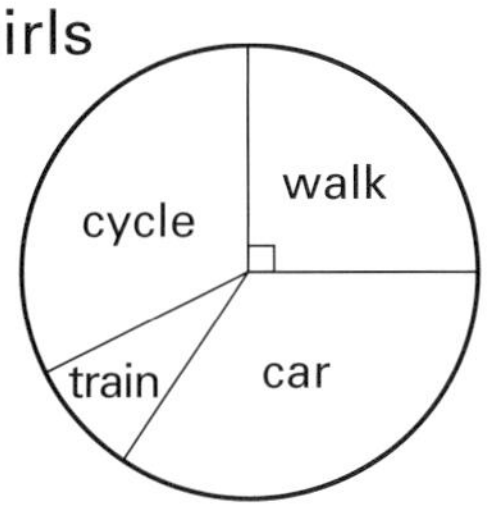

54 boys

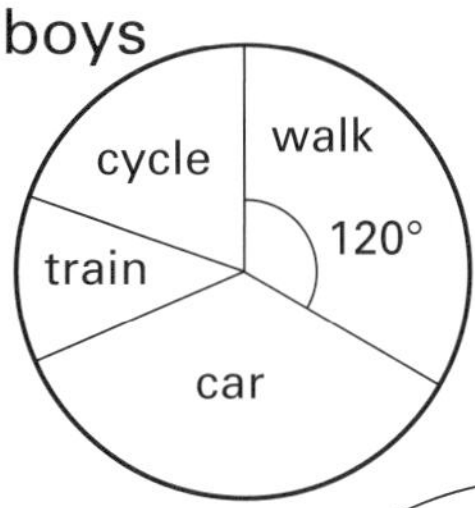

Monica says:

Monica is **wrong**. Explain why.

90° is a quarter of 360°.

So more girls walked than boys.

90° is a right angle, 120° is an obtuse angle.

He surveyed 76 girls but only 54 boys.

120° is a third of 360°.

$76 \div 4 = 19$, $54 \div 3 = 18$

4. The ratio of girls to boys in class 7Smt is 3:1.
Neil says:

Neil is **wrong**. Explain why.

The fraction is $\frac{1}{4}$.

There could be 21 girls and 7 boys.

For every 3 girls there is 1 boy.

So 3 out of every 4 pupils are girls and 1 is a boy.

5 Look at the diagram.

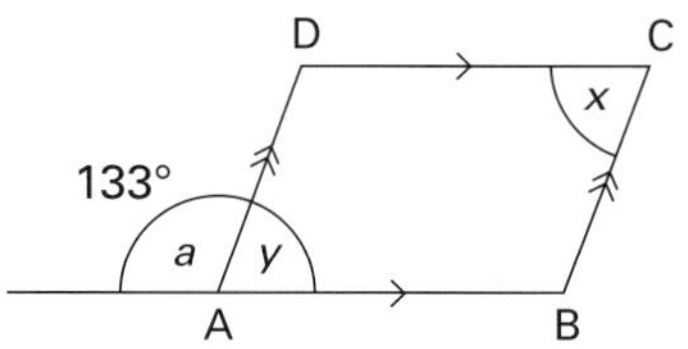

Explain why angle x = 47°.

The interior angles of a quadrilateral sum to 360°.	So $y = 180° - 133°$ which equals 47°.
Shape ABCD is a parallelogram.	Angles a and y are angles on a straight line.
So $x = y = 47°$.	The opposite angles in parallelogram are equal.

6 This is a 3-digit square number with a units digit of 4.

_ _ 4

Could its square root be a prime number?

Explain your answer.

The square root must be a 2 digit number.

The only even prime is 2 which is a one digit number.

A prime number is a number with only two factors: 1 and itself.

So the square root cannot be a prime number.

The only numbers that will square to give a number with a 4 in the units column are even.

Badger Publishing Limited
26 Wedgwood Way
Pin Green Industrial Estate
Stevenage
Hertfordshire SG1 4QF
Telephone: 01438 356907
Fax: 01438 747015
www.badger-publishing.co.uk
enquiries@badger-publishing.co.uk

Main Activity – Problem Solved!
Student Book 1
ISBN 1 84424 033 9

Publisher: David Jamieson
Editor: Paul Martin
Designer: Niki Bowers
Design project management: Hilary Davies
Illustrator: Juliet Breese
Characters by Tania Konstant

Printed in the UK